100

THINGS TO DO IN
SAN JOSE
BEFORE YOU
DIE

Edition

100

2nd Edition

THINGS TO DO IN
SAN JOSE
BEFORE YOU
DIE

SUSANNAH GREENWOOD

REEDY PRESS

Library of Congress Control Number: 2019940038

ISBN: 9781681062372

Design by Jill Halpin

Front cover image: Susannah Greenwood

Back cover image: Daniel Garcia

Printed in the United States of America
19 20 21 22 23   5 4 3 2 1

Please note that websites, phone numbers, addresses, and company names are subject to change or cancellation. We did our best to relay the most accurate information available, but due to circumstances beyond our control, please do not hold us liable for misinformation. When exploring new destinations, please do your homework before you go.

ACKNOWLEDGMENTS

My sincere thanks to Reedy Press, the San Jose Downtown Association, the City of San Jose, Visit San Jose, Evelyn Seto, and the people of San Jose—past, present, and future.

To all my family, friends, teachers, coaches, mentors, and guardians; thanks for making this a fascinating journey, one that continues to thrill and amuse me.

Pullman, Lincoln, and Paxton (the three-legged wonder cats present and past), you probably can't read this, but just in case, thanks for your supreme patience and purrs.

Thanks must also be extended to the internet, sunny days, the occasional adult beverage, tacos, wagging dog tails, flip-flops, dinosaurs, pennies, caffeine, my trusty Jeep, Pluto (you were robbed), Lasik eye surgery, Jason Statham, Fritter, the Doma-Cile, puns, Science, free parking, hats, and wanderlust.

CONTENTS

Arts and Entertainment

• •

Sports and Recreation

● ●

• •

Mind the Geek

FOREWORD

You can't possibly tell San Jose you only want 100 of its "things." That only 100 of these things inside or nearby its precious boundaries are things you need to do before you die. That's just nonsense. San Jose won't have it. No, San Jose won't listen because there are thousands of stories and delightful discoveries all around this tenth largest city in the United States.

So I told San Jose these were just the first 100 things to do. San Jose started to object, not liking to be told what to do (this clearly stemming from its years of pioneering and innovation), but I made my case. These 100 things, they're just suggestions. San Jose didn't totally buy it, but the protest seemed to subside. To explore San Jose properly, to really get in the spirit, get inside its head, you need to think like the founding visionaries. You can start with a plan, an idea, or inspiration (thus this book), but ultimately, the best way is to find your own path, a new way— your own way to San Jose.

The pages here are as much a love letter to the diverse and eclectic people that make up San Jose as they are a guide to its attractions, for you will meet amazing people while you mine these nuggets of fun and adventure. And I have to agree with San Jose on this point: you really can't fit all of them in a book.

• •

I hope the distinct and varied rhythms I've tried to capture on these pages—the cadence of San Jose's fascinating history, exciting present, and bright future—inspire you to explore to the beat of your own drum.

FOOD AND DRINK

TAKE ON
TACO TUESDAY

We take our tacos very, *very* seriously here. While we locals consider each day of the week equally appropriate for tacos, Tuesday is kind of the taco birthday of the week. From high end to hole in the wall, and from traditional to experimental, the taco is revered and interpreted pretty much 24/7. The only limit to the filling is your imagination. Time stops for the taco in San Jose— we even have an annual Taco Festival of Innovation. There are hundreds of places to get your taco fix, and each culture has its own take on this perfect little food.

Good for families

Authentic Traditional Fare

Araujo's Mexican Grill El Paisa
3070 Senter Rd., San Jose, 95111
408-300-0814, araujosmexicangrill.com

Angelou's Mexican Grill
21 N 2nd St. San Jose, 95113
408-971-2287, angelousmexicangrill.com

Luna Mexican Kitchen
1495 The Alameda, San Jose, 95126
408-320-2654, lunamexicankitchen.com

Exquisite Fish Tacos

Dia de Pesca
55 N Bascom Ave., San Jose, 95128
408-287-3722, pescasifood.com

For the More Exotic Palate

Zona Rosa
1411 The Alameda, San Jose, 95126
408-275-1411, zonarosadining.com

Taco Festival of Innovation
facebook.com/tacofestival

RELISH THE PERFECT DOG
AT MARK'S HOT DOG

Since 1936 the best hot dogs in San Jose (almost unanimously) have been prepared within the kooky and somewhat confusing walls of a 15-foot cement orange. Yes, you read that correctly. While the semi-spherical, ultra-iconic landmark moved from its original Alum Rock location to its current place on South Capitol in 2000, it remains the San Jose go-to spot for the dog of all dogs. Fans return again and again for that perfect snap you're looking for in a dog and all the chili, cheese, onions, and sauerkraut you can pile on a footlong masterpiece of days-gone-by meatiness. In an era when new dining establishments are unlikely to survive their first year, Mark's is proof that they DO make 'em like they used to and that's still appealing to and affordable for the masses. My only advice may be obvious: vegetarians, enter at your own risk.

Mark's Hot Dogs, 48 S Capitol Ave., San Jose, 95127
408-926-0923

Good for families

SAMPLE A BIT OF THE BIG EASY
AT THE POOR HOUSE BISTRO

I know you were just thinking, "Where can I park my krewe for a little down-home NOLA spice and laid-back music?" Don't be getting all mardi up in my gras; San Jose has you covered if you're craving Cajun. Slide on up to the Poor House Bistro and *laissez les bon temps rouler*. This converted Victorian with more outside than inside seating is a local favorite. Along with the expected traditional N'awlins faves like jambalaya, crawfish, and po'boys, the Creole Sunday brunch items, such as BBQ shrimp Benedict, will have you convinced you've been transported to the gulf. Add to that the best corn muffin on the entire planet and seven days a week of live jazz, blues, and rock, and you have your slice of Louisiana without trading in a single string of beads for it.

Poor House Bistro, 91 S Autumn St., San Jose, 95110
408-292-5837, poorhousebistro.com

PAIR FARM-FRESH FOOD WITH GORGEOUS VALLEY VIEWS
AT THE MOUNT HAMILTON GRANDVIEW RESTAURANT

Planning a romantic date. Ugh. Seriously, the struggle is real (for some of us more than others). I know that's not a super popular stance to take; after all, if it's meant to be, it *should* be easy. Sorry, I'm gonna call rubbish. Everyone has their own distinct rules about what makes a great date, and yet those rules can seemingly be completely tossed out for no discernible reason at any time, plunging a well-planned date into last date territory. That said, your odds at capturing all the romantic feels increase tenfold by reserving a table at the Mount Hamilton GrandView Restaurant. It has all the hallmarks of that date magic: epic (and I do mean EPIC) views of the entire Silicon Valley, a 1,500-foot vantage point for mind-blowing sunsets and star-gazing, an organic farm across the road where nearly everything they serve is grown (including the meat), the creative, constantly developing farm-driven menus, good-size portions, and substantial wine and cocktail offerings. Let the GrandView take some of that pressure off of you with its magical natural setting and delectable slow food, so you can focus on your slow *moves*. Let's maybe also just pretend I never wrote "so you can focus on your slow moves," if that'd be okay.

The Mount Hamilton GrandView Restaurant
15005 Mount Hamilton Rd., San Jose, 95140
408-251-8909, grandviewsanjose.com

TIP

During the 4th of July and New Year's Eve, fireworks displays from the entire valley can be seen from the outdoor patio if the weather is clear. Turn your date night up a notch with just such a spectacle, available to those who make an early reservation.

SAVOR THE MOMENT
AT THE EXQUISITE LE PAPILLON

Admittedly, Le Papillon's understated outside doesn't exude five-star dining, but its presentable yet modest exteriors are forgotten the moment you walk in the door. The flavors, the plating, the service, it's all top-notch with a wine list to die for. This is fine French cuisine with plenty of international and *Top Chef*–type flair. The serving sizes are surprisingly ample and the prices beyond reasonable, especially considering its culinary bliss. Please observe: this may be the only place you will not find a smartphone at the table. Yes, sadly, smartphones (and cell phones) are banned, so your food porn Instagrams will have to be replaced by actual, in-the-moment dining, and you'll have to tell your friends about the perfection of every dish using your words. Yes, it's frightening at first, then refreshing and totally worth it—once you cut the cord.

Le Papillon, 410 Saratoga Ave., San Jose, 95129
408-296-3730, lepapillon.com

"RAV ON"
AT BERTUCELLI'S LA VILLA DELICATESSEN

Ravioli. Done right, it's a pretty perfect little pillow of mouth happy, no? Especially when they're homemade, fresh, hot, right out of the pot, and smothered with freakishly amazing marinara. Comfort food times infinity. Ask anyone in San Jose where to get the best ravioli in town (and possibly in the universe) and with the exception of a few who'll say their Nonna, their answer is going to be La Villa. It's really a no-brainer. I mean, when one has a tab on their website dedicated just to ravioli orders, you know you're staring at a pretty legendary purveyor of ravioli. While the cheese ravs are delectably divine, the lobster, chicken, feta, and beef are all acclaimed, too. Incidentally, there's a reason you can purchase online up to twenty boxes of forty-eight ravioli at a time—the "all La Villa ravioli all the time" diet; it's totally a thing here.

Bertucelli's La Villa Delicatessen, 1319 Lincoln Ave., San Jose, 95125
408-295-7851, wglavilla.com

Good for families

SAVE A SWEET SHOP
DO DONUTS

In an age of emphasis on healthy eating and fad diets, you'd think the donut would be a sweet toothed dinosaur facing imminent extinction. Well, think again; donuts are here to stay. Far from being do-nots, donuts are clearly do's in San Jose. Sure there's been some evolution here and there; cronuts happened and vegan donutries occupy a space in the market, but this largely lardy, nostalgic favorite is clearly beloved despite its reputation for being an unfair majority of one's daily caloric intake. Almost as incendiary as the great pizza debate, everyone has their favorite donut shop and a thesis-length advocacy document stating why their preferred donut is by far the best in town. A warm, fresh donut with the perfect balance of airy fluff and sticky gooey glaze is an art worth preserving and perhaps the biggest selling points aside from obvious pastry quality is that the majority of donut shops are independent, family-owned, mom and pop shops that have been around for a long time. They're the kind of places that throw in free donut holes, only take cash (but give you the goods and just ask you to come back tomorrow with it if you only have credit cards with you), and will ask you how your dad or your daughter is doing. So really, it would appear, the karmic calories burned by supporting small donut businesses far exceed those "real" calories. Plus, I'm pretty sure the act of justifying the consumption of such fattening circles of OMG burns like 5,000 calories. Right? Right.

Happy Donuts, 1345 S Winchester Blvd., San Jose, 95128
408-871-1888

Tasty Donuts, 485 Saratoga Ave., San Jose, 95129
408-249-3755

Rollo's Donuts, 602 N 13th St., San Jose, 95112
408-294-7757, rollosdonuts.com

Vegan Donut and Cafe, 449 E Santa Clara St., San Jose, 95113
408-606-8664

Good for families

BRAVE THE SIX-LEGGED APPETIZERS
AT MEZCAL

Whether or not you need the extra liquid courage provided by Mezcal's notable collection of tequilas and mezcales in order to partake in the chapulines (fried grasshoppers sautéed with garlic, lime, and salt), the colorful restaurant serves both. If the owner, Adolfo, is there, he'll even give you a lesson on the differences between various tequilas and mezcales just in case that helps work up your nerve. Then again, if shots or six-legged things aren't your bag, the many other family recipes will certainly please the palate. Oaxacan cuisine has a French influence resulting from a large migration during the 1800s. Its unique blend of New World European and Old World indigenous flavors really sets it apart as a special dining experience (with or without an insect course). With three types of homemade moles, fresh guacamole made for you tableside, and Mexican desserts, there's no possibility you'll leave hungry or unhappy.

Mezcal, 25 W San Fernando St., San Jose, 95113
408-283-9595, mezcalrestaurantsj.com

9

FALL IN LINE
AT FALAFEL'S DRIVE-IN

When a restaurant is new, you can count on a certain amount of temporary, line-forming fanaticism. It's harder to write off a line after the first year or so of operation. What you cannot ignore is the line that has formed outside Falafel's Drive-In since it opened in 1966. I know. There's a lot going on with that name. It's a bit of a mystery. But wait, there's more. Besides homemade falafel and a variety of Middle Eastern menu items, what makes this place even more of an enigma is that you can get burgers and fries and even corn dogs here, too. The falafel is quite good, but let's shoot straight: there's something about a place called Falafel's Drive-In and fifty years of lining up that just has to be experienced.

Falafel's Drive-In, 2301 Stevens Creek Blvd., San Jose, 95128
408-294-7886, falafelsdrivein.com

Good for families

LIVE THE SWEET LIFE
AT PETERS' BAKERY

Since 1936, sweet teeth have been traveling miles to Peters' Bakery to partake of the magical baked goods that are created fresh, on-site each morning. This small, friendly bakery in Little Portugal was founded on hard work and a passion for carefully crafting desserts. Known especially for their burnt almond cake, which impresses even the most discerning taste buds, their authentic Portuguese sweet breads, éclairs, custards, and strawberry rings are also highly coveted. As the oldest family-run bakery in Silicon Valley, Peters' is nothing short of a San Jose institution. And in addition to lining the masses up in front of their own store, the impact of this historic business reaches far and wide by way of the hundreds of bakers who were trained by founder Tony Peters.

Peters' Bakery, 3108 Alum Rock Ave., San Jose, 95127
408-258-3529

TIP
Peters' Bakery is closed on Sundays and is cash only, so for optimal enjoyment make sure you arrive with plenty of the green stuff in addition to an empty stomach.

SCOUT OUT THE ORIGINAL STROMBOLI
AT TONY DI MAGGIO'S PIZZA

Wars have been started by claiming which establishment makes the best pizza and it's certainly not a battle I want to wage here. I mean, I'm not crazy. That said, stromboli is an entirely different matter, and I'll willingly insert myself into that debate right now. Hands down, Tony Di Maggio's Pizza, which opened in San Jose way back in 1977, is stromboli king. Tony's is most definitely the Home of the Original Stromboli and one of the best, if not the best, to boot. What is Stromboli? Glad you asked . . . ham, Italian sausage, salami, mustard, American cheese, and mozzarella cheese, all wrapped in pizza dough and topped with butter, oregano, black pepper, and homemade tomato sauce. It's a cornucopia of Italian zip, kick, crunch, and saucy, savory goodness developed by Tony during his time in New York and Pennsylvania. Even if it wasn't first, it'd still be molto tasty and well worth a visit.

3852 Monterey Hwy., San Jose, 95111
408-629-7775, tonydimaggiospizza.com

and also at
155 W San Fernando St., San Jose, 95113

TAKE YOUR SWEET OLD TIMEY
AT ORCHESTRIA PALME COURT

It must be the healthful ingredients in reasonable portions that sets Orchestria Palme Court apart from other restaurants. Of course, it could be that their old-fashioned soda fountain has something to do with it. Then again, it might be their no-rush, no-waitstaff, "stay all night if you want" approach to dining that's really bringing in the crowds. No. Wait. I wonder if the fact that they match their restaurant's musical focus to the local arts events going on around them has anything to do with their popularity. It might just be that within the rustic walls of the restored 1910 building there are over a dozen vintage player pianos, orchestrions, and jukeboxes, providing unparalleled old-timey ambiance. I know, it's all of the above.

Orchestria Palme Court, 27 E Williams St., San Jose, 95112
408-288-5606, orchestriapalmcourt.com

TIP
With its special concept comes even more special hours, so make sure to check whether they are open before you swing by.

GET SHAKEN AND STIRRED
AT THE FAIRMONT LOBBY LOUNGE

A menu with five hundred different martinis. This should pretty much sell the Fairmont Lobby Lounge experience in and of itself, don't you think? Five hundred. That's not a typo. Yes, this is a beautiful lounge. Yes, it's open late. Yes, this is a fine place to dance to live bands, watch sports, canoodle, or relax by live piano. But more importantly, there exists a menu of five hundred martinis. That's just martinis. The magical menu includes seventy pages of cocktails you can order. And here's the genius part: just in case you try to order all five hundred, the Fairmont San Jose also happens to be a hotel with over eight hundred rooms available for sleeping in. Many of them provide stunning views of the city, so you can always just stay the night. Five hundred, people! That's martini madness!

Fairmont Lobby Lounge, 170 S Market St., San Jose, 95113
408-998-1900, fairmont.com/san-jose/dining

DEVOUR AWARD-WINNING POKE
AT TIKI PETE

There are certainly days when sipping a tropical drink out of a pineapple and dining on award-winning ahi poke just seems like it's the answer to everything. I'm going to let you in on a secret. Sometimes it is, and Tiki Pete can hook you up, brah. For your fabulous fruit fix, order the mai tai or the piña colada, which are indeed served inside a hollowed out pineapple. Both the ahi and salmon poke are out of this world, but the extensive menu of authentic island dishes, like loco moco, Spam musubi, and kalua pork sliders, certainly makes you want to extend your culinary vacation. You can't help but go all macadamia nuts for this place.

Tiki Pete, 23 N Market St., San Jose, 95113
408-713-2900, tikipete.us

JOIN THE NEIGHBORHOOD
AT THE NAGLEE PARK GARAGE

The large communal tables on the patio of this tiny converted garage confidently declare that when you're at NPG, you're part of the neighborhood family. This new American, European influenced eatery with a small but sophisticated menu of comfort food, is a beautiful blend of community dish and outstanding dishes. A dog and kid-friendly destination with craft brews on tap always makes your visit to the Garage a warm and fuzzy one (especially with the tabletop fire pits used on chillier evenings). The seasonal risotto and polenta are highly recommended as is the Garage Burger. Note that the restaurant's popularity and limited seating makes this a good pick for those in the mood for a relaxed, no-rush, extended dining experience.

Naglee Park Garage, 505 E San Carlos St., San Jose, 95112
408-564-4111, nagleeparkgaragesanjose.cafeshousebiz.online

Good for families

LET YOUR TASTE BUDS TRAVEL
WITH A LITTLE ETHIOPIAN
IN LITTLE ETHIOPIA

Awesome tends to seek out other awesome. Look at the number of outstanding Ethiopian restaurants crowded into a very small section of West San Jose known unofficially as Little Ethiopia. This cuisine is not only brimming with flavor, but the way Ethiopian food is served and typically eaten embodies so many San Jose attitudes and values. The act of eating Ethiopian food is social, artistic, adventurous, steeped in ritual, efficient, a tad messy, and simultaneously humble and decadent. San Jose's plentitude of Ethiopian restaurant options range from the full traditional seating experience and sharing the entire meal, to a more Western style table arrangement with individual entrees, but all of them qualify as totally authentic when it comes to the actual food. Don't know your Doro Wat from your Tibs and Kitfo? Need to exchange the injera method for a fork? No worries; service with a smile and navigation through the nuances for those participating in their first Ethiopian meal is standard and fully complimentary.

Walia Ethiopian Cuisine
2208 Business Cir., San Jose, 95128
waliaethiopian.com

Kategna Ethiopian
1663 W San Carlos St., San Jose, 95128
408-216-9695, websitekategna.com

Zeni Ethiopian
1320 Saratoga Ave., San Jose, 95129
408-615-8282, zeniethiopianrestaurant.com

Selam Restaurant and Cafe
3120 Williams Rd., San Jose, 95117
selamrestaurantandcafe.com

Mudai Ethiopian Restaurant
503 W San Carlos St., San Jose, 95126
408-292-2282, mudaiethiopian-hub.com

Gojo Ethiopian
1261 W San Carlos St., San Jose, 95126
408-295-9546, gojoethiopianrestaurant.com

DELICIOUSLY ADDRESS ALL YOUR DIETARY PREFERENCES
AT MENDOCINO FARMS

There you are, chilling after a great day in San Jose with a group of friends or family and all of a sudden it's time to pick a place to eat. This should be an easy task in concept (you're all reasonable human beings after all), but as you start to assess the situation it becomes clear—you're going to need a major meal miracle. With one vegan, two vegetarians, one celiac, two picky eaters, three serious carnivores, four fierce foodies, one soy allergy, one person who says they don't care but-so-totally-does, and a dog who requires a patio, how can you possibly please half the group let alone everyone? You go back and forth and around in circles for what seems like an eternity with no solution in sight, and panic starts to set in. You teeter on the precipice of hangry, and the window with which you have the ability to function on any basic human level quickly begins to dissipate. It is then that the thought crosses your mind that you might die hungry. We've all been there. Never fear, your miracle menu is here and it's called Mendocino Farms. By far one of the most accommodating and scrumptious restaurants around, it exemplifies the California fresh culinary experience, providing delicious options for every dietary need without sacrificing one iota of flavor or creativity. Where else can you get a pork belly banh mi, a vegan organic house-smoked BBQ tempeh sandwich, a prosciutto and free-range chicken pesto sandwich, and Impossible vegan taco salad, and a chimichurri steak sandwich on a pretzel. That's just a sampling of the inventive and downright ambrosial choices (each clearly marked for ease of ordering) available. Plus, you order in line and they bring the food to you, so there's none of that bill splitting or waiting after the meal to further frustrate. Yes, you have the power to take the headache out of group dining and be hangry no more!

Mendocino Farms, 3090 Olsen Dr., Ste 150, San Jose, 95128
408-207-1390, mendocinofarms.com

Good for families

CELEBRATE OKTOBERFEST
EVERY MONTH AT TESKE'S GERMANIA

A list of things that make a good Oktoberfest: German beer served in giant steins. Insane helpings of sausage and schnitzel. Lederhosen. German hospitality. Really friendly strangers. A polka band that plays German drinking songs followed by Robin Thick, Lady Gaga, Miley Cyrus, Prince, Psy, Johnny Cash, and Frank Sinatra covers. Wait, what was that last one? Oh yes, it's the monthly visit of the Internationals to Teske's! A band—nay, an event—that makes this already genuine Bavarian getaway feel just like Oktoberfest, only with warmer temperatures and more frequent entertainment. By the conclusion of the night, you'll be amply satiated with authentic German food, you'll have learned all about German beer, you'll have a million new drinking buddies, and you may want to take the band home with you because they are so ever-loving adorable. If your cheeks are in need of a smile workout, get down to Teske's and fill up on Deutsche food and frivolity.

Teske's Germania, 255 N 1st St., San Jose, 95113
408-292-0291, teskes-germania.com

The Internationals
theinternationals.com

SAMPLE TERIYAKI AND TAIKO
AT THE OBON FESTIVAL

July brings to Japantown one of the most anticipated cultural festivals in San Jose (and there are a lot!). Obon is a comparatively intimate festival; however, there is no shortage of food. Gyoza, udon, sushi, tempura, pearl tea, giant vats of boiled corn on the cob, red bean cake called imagawayaki, and seemingly endless grilling pits full of teriyaki are only some of the festival favorites. The signage is clear and the layout of booths is efficient, allowing you less time in line and more eating and taking in the visual feast. Along with the appealing aroma of Japanese cuisine, the powerful boom of taiko (ensemble drumming on large Japanese drums) also fills the air. Seeing San Jose Taiko perform for their own community among the kimonos and festive lantern-lined streets really does make this a feast for all your senses.

San Jose Buddhist Church Betsuin, 640 N 5th St. at Jackson and Taylor,
San Jose, 95112
sjbetsuin.com/obon

San Jose Taiko, taiko.org

Good for families

SIP AND SURPASS
YOUR GRAPEST EXPECTATIONS

I bet you didn't know that the Santa Clara Valley is California's oldest continuously producing wine region, did you? Well before Napa entered the viniculture arena, this area was producing grapes for the missions. As a result, San Jose offers as many options for sipping fine wine as there are varietals. Copious wine bars, each with its own special mood and focus, can be found all over the city.

The folks at Divine Winery Tasting Room specialize in small batch, handcrafted wines with an emphasis on California and a few small, family-owned international wines. If you taste one you enjoy, you can purchase a bottle on the spot. The owners are friendly and knowledgeable and eager to help you discover your favorites.

Village California Bistro and Wine Bar in Santana Row is the place for rare and hard to find wines no matter the region. They excel at pairing and offer 400 full bottles, 80+ half-bottles, 30 wines by the glass, and typically more than 9 different wine flights. And maybe best of all, every Monday is half price wine night, and any bottle under $100 (210 to choose from) is . . . you guessed it, half off.

The tasting room for J. Lohr Winery is an excellent option for sampling California's "grapest." In true San Jose spirit, no appointment is needed and no fee is charged for tastings (except for Cuvée Series or limited J. Lohr wines).

If you're looking for a winery tour fifteen minutes from downtown San Jose, the historic Testarossa Winery perches in the Los Gatos Hills. With stunning vineyard views, cellar cave tours, a tasting room, and a gorgeous patio shaded by ancient sycamore trees, this is the essence of vini, vidi, vino.

Divine Winery Tasting Room, 40 Post St., San Jose, 95113
650-465-5468, divinewinerics.com

Village California Bistro and Wine Bar, 378 Santana Row, #1035,
San Jose, 95128
408-248-9091, thevillagebistro.net

J. Lohr San Jose Wine Center, 1000 Lenzen Ave., San Jose, 95126
408-918-2160, jlohr.com

Testarossa Winery, 300 College Ave., Los Gatos, 95030
408-354-6150, testarossa.com

CONSUME YOUR WEIGHT
IN PHO AND BANH MI

As home to the largest Vietnamese population outside of Vietnam, San Jose knows a thing or two about the culinary traditions of this culture. The highly sought-after banh mi (Vietnamese sandwich) and pho (noodle soup) are more "tame" samples of the cuisine that have been embraced and are enjoyed by pretty much the whole city. While banh mi shops are almost as common as cafés, Lee's Sandwiches and Dakao are two solid options giving you lots of choices for fillings. For pho, Bun Bo Hue An Nam boasts a stellar reputation backed by "pho-nomenal" taste. For the more adventurous gastronome who is ready to taste first and find out what it was you ate later, an extreme quest awaits you at the Grand Century Mall, which boasts more than two hundred unique Vietnamese shops, including the South Asian food court of your dreams.

Lee's Sandwiches, 260 E Santa Clara St., San Jose, 95113
408-286-8808, leesandwiches.com

Dakao, 98 E San Salvador St., San Jose, 95112
408-286-7260, dakaosj.wix.com/dakao

Bun Bo Hue An Nam, 740 Story Rd., San Jose, 95112
408-993-1755

Grand Century Mall, 111 Story Rd., San Jose, 95112

Good for families

MANGIA YOUR WAY
THROUGH 1956 AT ORIGINAL JOE'S

Even if you were alive in the '50s or never wondered what it was like, Original Joe's is a perfect and delicious destination. It also happens to be a totally surreal leap back in time. This isn't a kitsch, gimmicky replication 1950s; OJ's is the real deal. A totally authentic Italian '50s eatery run by the same family that opened it in 1956, this iconic restaurant has retained just about all of its vintage flair. Décor, menu, regulars, service; it's a serious wormhole-type trip and a yummy one at that. Joe's Special, veal parmigiana, and a meatball sub grace the gigantic menu, and the plates of pasta are as big as your head. With meals served by waiters in tuxedos and the distinct sound of Italian being spoken in the highly visible kitchen, it's the kind of place where (despite being totally family friendly) you'd expect Tony Soprano to walk in any minute. Or Dean Martin. Or, quite possibly, Marty McFly.

Original Joe's, 301 S 1st St., San Jose, 95113
408-292-7030, originaljoes.com

Good for families

JUST CHILL OUT
ON THE PATIO AT THE
SAN PEDRO SQUARE MARKET

Sometimes you need a nice big outdoor space to just chill out. And sometimes you want to bring your dog to that place. Or your kids. Or both. And you don't really want to move more than about one hundred steps all day, which means you need lots of food and drink options in sight. You know, a pizza place, crepes, falafel, small-batch ice cream, tacos (obviously), Nepali steamed dumplings (called momo), Pho, and Venezuelan arepa, something of everything. And then certainly there are times when you want to just chill with beer. Lots of types of beer. Like, lots. And sometimes you'd like this patio of your dreams to have live music, trivia nights, free movie nights, or whiskey tastings. And big screens playing the sports games. Yeah. That. So sometimes you go to the San Pedro Square Market, and you just live the dream, man.

San Pedro Square Market, 87 N San Pedro St., San Jose, 95110
408-817-9435, sanpedrosquaremarket.com

Good for families

EAT YOUR BIG, FAT, GREEK HEART OUT
AT THE SAN JOSE GREEK FESTIVAL

If there were room (and if I had the talent), I'd write an entire Homeric poem about the San Jose Greek Festival. Oh loukoumades, oh gyros, oh baklava, souvlaki, moussaka, and spanakopita, get in my belly. This is a festival that serves up food cooked by local families with recipes passed down for generations. Greek culture is an ancient one, and they have had a few years to perfect things. This is your grandmother's melomakarona, and that's a good thing. People have been known to fast the week before, just to make sure they have room for the generous assortment of homemade delicacies. Round out your day (and your stomach) with lively bouzouki and surrounded by award-winning dancers, and you'll leave well versed and ready for next year.

St. Nicholas Greek Orthodox Church, 1260 Davis St., San Jose, 95126
408-246-2770, saintnicholas.org/greek-festival

Good for families

INDULGE
AT ADEGA

Tucked away in a small and casual, but chic and modern room in East San Jose, sits the city's first restaurant ever awarded the coveted Michelin Star. Adega's star shines bright in Little Portugal and does the neighborhood, San Jose, and Portuguese cuisine proud, by serving simple yet sophisticated, unpretentious (and likely new-to-you) dishes paired with exquisite Portuguese wines. The seasonal chef's tasting menu in particular makes for a phenomenal and decadent night out, allowing you to leave the impossible task of decision making to the experts and giving you an exceptional introduction to the meat and fish forward dishes central to the specific region's flavor. It also makes the bill splitting easy so you can pour yourself into your taxi sooner at the end of a VIP (Very Indulgent Portuguese) evening. Reservations are virtually essential and you'll want to budget in advance for a second and third visit.

Adega, 1614 Alum Rock Ave., San Jose, 95116
408-926-9075, adegarest.com

Veggielution, 647 S King Rd., San Jose, 95116
408-634-3276, veggielution.org

TIP

Each summer the urban farm Veggielution partners with Adega chefs Jessica Carreira and David Costa for their farm-to-table fEAST fundraiser. It's a fantastic way to enjoy Adega, take advantage of the gorgeous California weather, get in a barn dance, and support a vital community organization doing important work for East San Jose.

WET YOUR WHISTLE
AT SILICON VALLEY BEER WEEK

While I'm sure many dedicate more than just a week for paying homage to the frosty malt goddess, Silicon Valley makes a special point to revere the fermented beverage deity during Silicon Valley Beer Week. With scores of participating pubs, breweries, microbreweries, and individual beer makers, this event is an educational one, addressing all your burning beer questions. Which beers go with ice cream? What secret ingredient or technique will transform your home brew from meh to marvelous? With an array of beer-food pairings, beer-infused treats, expert panels, and ask-the-brewer opportunities, SVBW is not only an opportunity to discover the legitimate plethora of craft beer offerings popping up all over, but an insight into the new local movement stemming from a region with such a rich brewing history.

Silicon Valley Beer Week
svbeerweek.com

JUST A *SMALL* SAMPLING OF SAN JOSE'S BUSTLING BREW-LIFE AND SVBW PARTICIPATING BUSINESSES

Clandestine Brewing
980 S 1st St., Ste B, San Jose, 95110
408-520-0220, clandestinebrewing.com

Hapa's Brewing Company
460 Lincoln Ave., Ste 90, San Jose, 95126
408-982-3299, hapasbrewing.com

Strike Brewing
2099 S 10th St., Ste 30, San Jose, 95112
650-714-6983, strikebrewingco.com

Camino Brewing Co.
718 S 1st St., San Jose, 95113
408-352-5331, caminobrewing.com

Good Karma Artisan Ales & Cafe
37 S 1st St., San Jose, 95113
408-294-2694, goodkarmavegancafe.com

Uproar Brewing Company
439 S 1st St., San Jose, 95113
408-673-2266, uproarbrewing.com

Forager Tasting Room & Eatery
420 S 1st St., San Jose, 95172
408-831-2433, sjforager.com

O'Flaherty's Irish Pub
25 N San Pedro St., San Jose, 95110
408-947-8007, oflahertyspub.com

Trials Pub
265 N 1st St., San Jose, 95113
408-947-0497, trialspub.com

21 and over only if partaking in alcohol;
please drink responsibly.

ARTS AND ENTERTAINMENT

TELL WEDNESDAY
YOU CAN'T WAIT FOR THE WEEKEND AND HEAD TO CAFÉ STRITCH

A balance of casual, hip ambiance (devoid of pretension), well-crafted food, and noticeably absent inflated prices, Café Stritch is a friendly, laid-back, authentically cool space. This seat-and-serve-yourself venue has large exposed-brick walls and reclaimed-wood floors, and brings in packed houses for jazz artists who are both big and not-quite-yet-big deals. The vibe is chill and well-behaved, and one of the nicest things about it (aside from their seriously delicious mac and cheese) is the all-ages, diverse crowd that always seems to assemble. The music connects all walks of life and this watering hole, with style and hospitality to spare, feels like home. When Wednesday comes, and you can't wait for the weekend to start, here is where you will find your people.

Café Stritch, 374 S 1st St., San Jose, 95113
408-280-6161, cafestritch.com

TIP
Look for Buck Hill Productions and Silicon Valley Shakespeare's ShakesBEERience—a play reading showcasing San Jose's outside-the-box/bar/Bard thinking. Actors stand on the bar, sit in patron laps, and drink along with the audience as they recite! Upcoming experiences at Stritch: www.svshakespeare.org

CHALK IT UP
TO AWESOME AT THE LUNA PARK CHALK ART FESTIVAL

For many, the smell and feel of chalk is extremely nostalgic. Whether used at school or to doodle on driveways growing up, there's something wonderfully innocent and youthful about it. It stays with you and almost beckons you to dream. These same feelings of possibilities and creativity are at the core of the Luna Park Chalk Art Festival, and there is absolutely no limit to the subjects and styles that are represented at this free neighborhood event. Amateurs and professionals alike, side by side, take to the pavement grid to create fleeting, temporary masterpieces! Post-festival chalk sales have been known to spike considerably, as viewing the hundreds of squares has a way of sparking widespread inspiration.

Backesto Park, 651-699 Empire St., San Jose, 95112
lunaparkchalkart.org

Good family activity

THINK DEEP THOUGHTS
AT THE SAN JOSE INSTITUTE OF
CONTEMPORARY ART (ICA)

I'm the first to admit that sometimes I don't always "get" visual art, especially the more modern pieces; they tend to confuse me. I know I'm not alone. That being said, the opportunity to view conceptually challenging yet visually compelling art is still extremely appealing. If you're in the same boat as I am, drop your anchor at the ICA. They kind of live for compelling and challenging and are there to show you the best of the best in contemporary trends. Perhaps the greatest advantage of the institute (aside from the exhibits) is the fact that it's not a sprawling museum where you feel rushed and overwhelmed. The ICA gives you the time and space you need to reflect on what you are seeing, which, if you're like me, may take a bit of time.

ICA, 560 S 1st St., San Jose, 95113
408-283-8155, sjica.org

GET REEL
AT CINEQUEST FILM FESTIVAL

San Jose has a long history of being first. We're somehow genetically predisposed to early adoption, I think. One of the ways we get to feed our beta-testing sensibilities is the Cinequest Film Festival, one of the finest, friendliest, and most unpretentious film festivals in existence. For over a quarter of a century, Cinequest has been presenting a spectacular lineup of more than two hundred films spanning a two-week period each February and March. They inspire the next generation of filmmakers and their community with independent and foreign film screenings, many of which are world and/or U.S. premieres. They've also been celebrating the mavericks of the industry by hosting conversations with well-known actors, directors, writers, critics, and even technology innovators who develop new kinds of cinematic storytelling. There's a real sense of collective joy when passionate filmgoers sit next to passionate filmmakers, and the power of film is applauded at the conclusion of each screening.

Various locations downtown and in Redwood City
cinequest.org

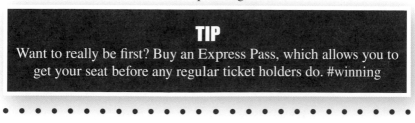

TIP
Want to really be first? Buy an Express Pass, which allows you to get your seat before any regular ticket holders do. #winning

PUT IT IN PARK
AT THE CAPITOL DRIVE-IN

Raise your hand if you have a better sound system in your car than in your house. Now, keep it up if your car is more comfortable than your living room. That's what I thought. There's a retro charm to a drive-in cinema for sure, but in some cases it's a pretty high-tech way to see a movie. The Capitol Drive-In sets you up with the current blockbusters in all-digital projection, plus double features rain or shine on the cheap, and you can't really beat that. Bring your own food or buy from the concession stand; enjoy from inside your vehicle or tailgate. What's not to like? Okay, you can put your hand down now.

West Wind Capitol 6 Drive-In, 3630 Hillcap Ave., San Jose, 95136
408-226-2251, westwinddi.com/locations/capitol

Good family activity

GO ALL ACCESS
AT THE SAN JOSE JAZZ SUMMER FEST

It would be impossible for me to explain just how big a deal the San Jose Jazz Summer Fest is. Like, thirteen stages impossible. But here's what you need to know. Hands down the best way to experience this massive three-day festival is to go all the way. Get a hotel room well in advance, get plenty of sleep the month before, build up your dance muscles and maybe your alcohol tolerance, and get that VIP all-access pass. Going VIP gives you first priority access to smaller stage events that fill up fast, front of stage access, shaded seating, and unlimited food and drink. This is the way to take in big-name headliners playing the main stage, up-and-coming artists in small club performances, the New Orleans style Big Easy Parade, Jazz Mass, Gospel Brunch, Jazz Jams, swing and salsa lessons, and more.

San Jose Jazz Summer Fest
summerfest.sanjosejazz.org

San Jose Jazz
sanjosejazz.org

TIP
Can't wait for summer? San Jose Jazz holds a smaller Winter Fest around March and sponsors a number of other one-off music events year-round.

MAKE A BEELINE FOR THE FELINES
AT THE DANCING CAT CAFE

If you believe the internet (and why wouldn't you?), there's no question who runs the world. Cats. The Dancing Cat understands this truth and caters to the large and excitable population of kitty zealots with their fur-bulous cat café. This brightly colored room of yay lodges eight to twelve adoptable, squee-worthy fur-babies and accommodates up to twelve human furophiles at a time. Have trouble catching that red dot at work today? No problem; unwind surrounded by a species that demands you leave your worries at the door and give them your undivided attention—until they vaguely indicate they're over it of course. TDC provides a soothing space to chill and indulge your fur fix even if you aren't looking to adopt. Is there anything better than relaxing in a cozy room, sipping a warm beverage, and raining adoration on your new BFFs (best feline friends?) The answer is no. Psych! The answer is: It DOES get better because TDC also hosts Mew-sic Night, Purr Yoga, cat henna tattoo parties, cat origami, and other purr-fect happenings with kitties. It's a meow-nificent time for all!

The Dancing Cat, 702 E Julian St., San Jose, 95112
408-459-9644, thedancingcat.org

WARNING!!!

Visiting The Dancing Cat
has led to over four hundred
cat adoptions since their initial
2015 opening including fur-ever
home matches made with several
people who "definitely did
not want a cat under any
circumstances."

RAGE ON DURING ARTRAGE
AT THE SAN JOSE MUSEUM OF ART

The San Jose Museum of Art is undoubtedly a grand excursion anytime, with its gorgeous layout and stunning collections. But one of the most delightful times to visit is during ArtRage. Every few months, this after-hours gathering combines your full-access gallery viewing with music, themed activities, shopping, a bit of wine, DIY art activities, lectures, and other cool surprises. It's a fun, eclectic, hip, but by no means necessarily young crowd that attends, and the energy and activities of the night pair well with the current exhibits. ArtRage is a fresh, relaxed, and more immersive approach to the museum for the avid art lover, the newbie, and everyone in between.

San Jose Museum of Art, 110 S Market St., San Jose, 95113
408-271-6840, sjmusart.org

EXPERIENCE ENTERTAINMENT
THAT'S A CUT ABOVE THE REST
AT 3BELOW THEATERS & LOUNGE

It's oft been said you can't have it all, but 3Below Theaters & Lounge not only totally debunks that myth, it virtually holds a daily parade for all the things of awesome going on under its roof. Live theater (both touring and locally produced), live music and cabaret nights, independent films (classic and first run, including documentaries), family sing-alongs of movies like *Grease* and *The Sound of Music*, and competitive improv brought to you by the wacky professionals of ComedySportz. Yes, Virginia, there IS a Santa Claus, and there is also a neighborly gathering place in downtown San Jose, where everyone is welcome and all are encouraged to be entertained in a multitude of ways. Quality is high and prices are surprisingly kind on your budget, making this a super place for families to soak in some culture, clowning, and community.

3Below Theaters & Lounge, 288 S Second St., San Jose, 95113
408-404-7711, 3belowtheaters.com

Good for families

MAKE IT A TRIPLE PLAY
AT SAN JOSE STAGE, CITY LIGHTS, AND NORTHSIDE THEATRE COMPANY

Bigger is not always better, and this may never be more true than when it comes to live theater. Theater is, after all, scalable, and sometimes a small theater—one, say, in the ninety-nine-seat range—can connect with you on a level that a larger one (in both seats and budget) may not. San Jose provides a varied performing arts experience with its myriad of intimate, but no less professional, theaters. What these theaters lack in seats they make up for in talent, creativity, technical ingenuity, and in most cases the absence of those annoying body mics. Proximity breeds nuanced, natural movement, the ability to hear a real whisper, and maybe even get a little bit of actor spit on you. San Jose Stage, City Lights Theater Company, and Northside Theatre Company all provide full seasons of thought-provoking, compelling entertainment with the sweet vantage point of never being more than ten rows away from the action.

San Jose Stage Company, 490 S 1st St., San Jose, 95113
408-283-7142, thestage.org

City Lights Theater Company, 529 S 2nd St., San Jose, 95112
408-295-4200, cltc.org

Northside Theatre Company, 84 E Williams St., San Jose, 95116
408-288-7820, northsidetheatre.com

BANISH YOUR BLUES
AT JJ'S LOUNGE

For decades JJ's was a secluded dive bar on the outskirts of town that specialized in blues and basic bar offerings. It hugged that line between respectable and ever-so-slightly seedy, but it largely went unnoticed by everyone outside the blues scene. A change in management has seen the live music traditions upheld and expanded, while the decor and ambiance of the lounge have transformed into a more upscale, craft cocktail and bottle service, club vibe. The blues offerings are still solid and there's a consistent lineup of supplemental rock, pop, jazz, and DJ music, with karaoke thrown in just to keep things interesting. Its small footprint keeps it friendly and relaxed with a motley mix of college students and the more mature, pre-renovation faithful fan base making up the majority of the clientele. The common ground here is good music and JJ's continues to provide a place for musicians to help you banish your blues.

3439 Stevens Creek Blvd., San Jose, 95117
408-785-0890, jjslounge.com

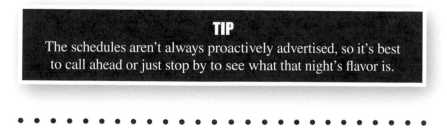

TIP
The schedules aren't always proactively advertised, so it's best to call ahead or just stop by to see what that night's flavor is.

FIND AN AUDIENCE
AT OPEN MIC NIGHT

Move over *American Idol*. Take a number *X Factor*. *The Voice*, who? San Jose is a mecca for budding artists, and pretty much any night of the week you can take in an open mic featuring a parade of potential next big things. From rock and acoustic folk, to opera and classical guitar, and even stand-up comedy, the local and independent coffee houses are full of opportunities to hear the talent of tomorrow over delicious liquid libation. Supportive spectators are always welcomed, and if the spirit moves you, sign up and show 'em what you've got.

Caffe Frascati, 315 S 1st St., San Jose, 95113
408-287-0400, caffefrascati.com

Cafe Lift, 5883 Eden Park Place, San Jose, 95138
cafeliftsj.com

Hub's Coffee, 630 Blossom Hill Rd., Suite 50, San Jose, 95123
408-622-8304, hubscoffee.com

Crema Coffee Roasting, 1202 The Alameda, San Jose, 95126
408-320-2215

South Bay Guitar Society, Vineland Branch Public Library,
1450 Blossom Hill Rd., San Jose, 95118
sbgs.org

LUNCH AND LEARN
WITH NOON ARTS AND LECTURES

The lunch hour is often times squandered with the exclusive act of feeding one's pie hole. We seem to be conditioned on some Pavlovian level to solely tend to those functions considered biologically necessary as soon as 12 o'clock rolls around. But what if we could nurture our souls and massage our creative synapse during that same time frame? And just like that, you can. Okay the lunch itself isn't free (we all know there's no such thing as that; you'll need to bring the food yourself), but the soul-stirring, brain-stimulating portion of your lunch hour costs nada when you attend a Noon Arts and Lectures presentation. Frequent Fridays and the occasional Thursday find you in various downtown venues (in and of themselves entertaining) privy to behind-the-scenes sneak peeks and mini-concerts featuring solo piano artists, acoustic guitar, internationally acclaimed quartets, chamber trios, award-winning poets, and even Gilbert & Sullivan. With opportunity for a truly well-balanced meal in every sense of the word, you'll never be able to just eat lunch again.

noonartsandlectures.org

Good family activity

VISIT THE DRAMATIC PAST
OF FOUR HISTORIC THEATERS
ALL INSIDE TWO CITY BLOCKS

It's kind of a crime to lump four gorgeous historic theaters into one must-see, but these sister theaters have been through a lot over the years and are now bonded together by their majestic pasts and blindingly bright futures. These ladies have aged gracefully and proved that age is just a number.

Beyond elegant, the California Theatre is a renovated art deco movie house and now hosts professional opera, symphony, dance, and silent films. Every inch of her is decadent, making her a coveted wedding venue.

The San Jose Center for the Performing Arts (CPA) is the place to be for Broadway touring shows and Symphony Silicon Valley. The 1972 building was built by the Frank Lloyd Wright Foundation and boasts a plethora of groovy circular architectural elements throughout.

The Rolling Stones, the Who, Morrissey, Frank Sinatra, Barbra Streisand, the Moody Blues, Bob Dylan . . . yeah, they've all played the San Jose Civic, and after its recent multi-million-dollar renovation, this city landmark is rocking so hard, Betty White is jealous.

The charming and intimate Montgomery Theater, built in 1936, plays home to Children's Musical Theater (CMT) San Jose, where several stars of Broadway got their start. She may be smaller than her other siblings at 475 seats, but she delivers a powerful theatrical punch.

Information on All Four Theaters
www.sanjosetheaters.org

California Theatre
345 S 1st St., San Jose, 95113

CPA
255 Almaden Blvd., San Jose, 95113

San Jose Civic
135 W San Carlos, San Jose, 95113

Montgomery Theater
271 S Market, San Jose, 95113

WALK THE WALK
AT SOUTH FIRST FRIDAYS

San Jose's SoFA (South of First Area) District is at the center of San Jose's creative pulse and, through its largely organic, grassroots collaboration, has transformed into its own exciting destination. Since 2005, the first Friday of the month (except January and July) has served as a collective display of the district's unique and ever-evolving arts scene. During the art walk a dozen exquisite and eclectic gallery doors are thrown open until midnight, free to the public. Many have demonstrations, artist receptions, libations, hands-on activities, and other entertainment, but the art doesn't just stay in the places you'd expect. During South First Fridays in particular, you'll find live music and art exhibits at corporate offices and yoga studios too. While a visit to SoFA is always a blast (especially with the SoFA Market food court there in the center of it all to satiate all your particular comestible hankerings), the art walk is an efficient and immensely satisfying way to experience a ton of art in just a few hours.

South First Friday Art Walk
southfirstfridays.com

SubZERO Festival
subzerofestival.com

SoFA Market, 387 S 1st St., San Jose, 95113
408-642-5270, sofamarketsj.com

Good family activity

TIP

Each June, South First Friday is taken to a whole new level when they block off the streets, bring in stages, open a beer garden, and welcome blocks of artists' booths. Live body painting, performance art, fashion shows, art cars, mural painting—anything and everything is possible, and it's a feast they call the SubZERO Festival.

GET DOWN
WITH THE DOWNTOWN PUBLIC ART WALK

Just a quick stroll around downtown and it's easy to see why San Jose was ranked one of America's Top Art Places. From the airport and the convention center to city hall and San Jose State University, there are hundreds of amazing public art installations. Over the years we've seen the Downtown Doors program and the Art Box Project SJ transform utility doors and utility boxes with art by local high school students and professional artists. Murals, phantom galleries that appear in the windows of unleased office space, and even interactive art make it impossible to go a single block without running into urban masterpieces. Painting the town has become a mission for many and the results are lighting up spaces and faces across the city. Grab a map or explore organically.

Downtown Public Art Walk
sanjose.org/listings/downtown-san-jose-public-art-walk

The Exhibition District
exhibitiondistrict.com

Downtown Doors
sjdowntown.com/foundation

Art & Murals of Downtown
and BEYOND
codeforsanjose.com/heartofthevalley

Eco-City Cycles
408-771-7723, ecocitycycles.com

Good family activity

TIP

If you want to cover more ground, one of the best ways to see the city and its art is to hire an Eco-City Cycles pedicab (for up to four people) and take in the art and the open air with an amiable cycle guide. It's safe, fun, and a great way to get about, plus you can negotiate your fee up front for custom trips.

HAVE
YOUR VISION ADJUSTED
BY TEATRO VISIÓN

What is perhaps most significant about Teatro Visión is that they describe their productions as a service to the community. This Chicano theater company is deeply invested in telling stories and entertaining its audience, but also in nurturing the next generation of community leaders and cultural ambassadors in their audience. Checking their egos at the door and harnessing the arts to inspire a better civic family, this group excels at presenting a phenomenal blend of specifically Chicano and Latino narratives that are also universally engaging and powerful. Many of them are performed partly or entirely in Spanish with supertitles, but even if you don't speak a word of Spanish, the talent and production values are so high caliber that they easily transcend any perceived language barrier. As an added bonus, most of the performances are held at the School of Arts and Culture at Mexican Heritage Plaza, a stunning modern facility with tremendous presence and technical capability.

Teatro Visión
408-294-6621, teatrovision.org

School of Arts & Culture at Mexican Heritage Plaza, 700 Alum Rock Ave.,
San Jose, 95116
408-794-6250, schoolofartsandculture.org

BECOME AN ART COLLECTOR
FOR $2 A POP AT KALEID GALLERY

Think art collecting is only for the wealthy? Think again. Luckily, you don't need to be making a Silicon Valley sized income to become a certified buyer and patron, thanks to the Kaleid Gallery and its beyond awesome $2 Tuesdays. Rock up to their sixty-plus-member art co-op and explore sculpture, collage, painting, jewelry, photographs, and art from just about every medium. Smaller works, sketches, and prints by the artists are set at just $2 for this monthly event, which often has demonstrations, activities, or performances scheduled too. You see, sometimes it is the little things that count.

Kaleid Gallery, 88 S 4th St., San Jose, 95113
408-271-5151, kaleidgallery.com

Good family activity

CELEBRATE A SPACE FOR THE AGES
AT THE ART BOUTIKI

The availability of all-ages venues, especially those with programming appropriate for teens, is not always a business model able to find sustained success. Learner's permits rarely equate to big business and the ability to pay Silicon Valley rents. Thankfully, Dan Vado has made it his mission to provide just such a space while somehow miraculously making the math work out, too. More impressively, he has done so for years. Dan and his company SLG Publishing launched the careers of many well-known comic book creators including Jhonen Vasquez, Evan Dorkin, Gene Luen Yang, and John "Derf" Backderf, so it would make sense that his Geekeasy dubbed The Art Boutiki is part comic book store. Teens (and those full-fledged adult types who drive them to events, pay for them in some cases, and also attend events with them) also like music, so the Boutiki is set up with a stage that serves as an incubator for local bands (of all ages) as well as touring ones. We all need to snack, so there's a cafe in there to help keep everyone's stomachs from growling during the events. The rest of the venue is filled with an eclectic mix of indy books, small press titles, t-shirts, CDs, collectibles, and records. Art Boutiki is a casual hangout with multiple monthly all-ages shows including a Jazz Jam and an open mic (both free). Dan keeps it accessible and fun with popular niche events like the regular Drink and Draw nights, which invite folks to come sketch, color, doodle, and draw alongside featured artists while DJs spin vinyl tunes for inspiration. It's really just the epitome of a safe and laid-back, judgment-free, inclusive, mellow, cozy, and creative zone. It's hella cool (as the kids say), but more important, this small space with a big soul occupies a special place in the appreciative hearts of many residents for opening its doors to the needy and deserving teens.

The Art Boutiki, 44 Race St., San Jose, 95126
408-971-8929, artboutiki.com

Good for families

MAKE AN
ARTS DISCOVERY
AT THE TABARD THEATRE

On the second floor of the historic Farmers Union Building, surrounded by exposed wood beams and century-old brick, sits a theater with approximately 150 of the most comfortable, wide leather seats with perfect views of the stage. On that stage a full season is produced by the resident (and also managing) Tabard Theatre Company. When the Tabard Theatre Company isn't performing their own full season of new works, musicals, and family-appropriate theater, that stage hosts Nerd Nite Silicon Valley, comedy, film, dance, and many other events befitting "the destination for arts discovery in Silicon Valley." To the left of the stage is a really huge and gorgeous bar. Altogether, the Tabard Theatre is the kind of space that may inspire a feeling of love at first sight. With its great atmosphere and diverse lineup most nights of the week, it's a tough act to follow.

The Tabard Theatre, 29 N San Pedro St., San Jose, 95110
408-679-2330, tabardtheatre.org

Good family activity

SHARE THE LAUGHTER
AT THE SAN JOSE IMPROV

Across the country, options for comedy in small venues are disappearing at alarming rates. It's no joke; with the strain of a tour schedule and the lucrative lure of film and TV, live comedy is in many ways a dying art. Your options are steadily becoming either shelling out beaucoup bucks for a stadium tour to see a microscopic Amy Schumer from the nosebleeds or viewing the latest special from your living room, which begs the question: If you laugh at the punchline and no one hears you, is it still funny? San Jose takes its shenanigans very seriously. One might even say it doesn't take its stand-up sitting down. Indeed, it operates under the strict philosophy that laughter is best shared, and its commitment to comedy is demonstrated beautifully in the superbly restored 1904 Jose Theater. With a long history of highlighting humor and a legacy that includes Vaudeville (and an appearance by Houdini even), this beautiful, balconied, 450-seat theater has been the home of the San Jose Improv (which has, in turn, played host to the very best comedians) since 2002. From up-and-coming comics to regular weekly headliners like David Spade, Gabriel Iglesias, Whitney Cummings, Bob Saget, Mo'Nique, Anjelah Johnson, Carlos Mencia, and Bobby Lee, this is the house hilarity built and where the collective joy of shared laughter thrives.

San Jose Improv, 62 S 2nd St., San Jose, 95113
408-280-7475, improv.com/sanjose

SPORTS AND RECREATION

BIKE, BLADE, AND BOARD
AT VIVA CALLESJ

How many times have you been sitting in traffic and shouted up to the heavens, "I wish everyone would just get off my road"? Three times, was it? Well, the Viva CalleSJ deities heard you, and they've decided to grant you your wish at least once every year. Yes, it takes a logistical feat of herculean proportions to shut down six miles of San Jose's city streets and transform them into the coolest-ever open street party, but you deserve it. You deserve the opportunity to glide down the street free of vehicles with 100,000 of your neighbors on bikes, boards, skates, and on foot for five hours discovering businesses you never knew existed. You deserve to have intersections with live performances, games, and raffles. You absolutely deserve the chance to cycle up a freeway cloverleaf sans fear of getting run over and to finally try one of those trendy scooters without running into a car. You also 100% deserve to participate in a special Pokemon Go Scavenger Hunt. Yes, you deserve at least one day a year of not sitting in traffic and instead celebrating exercise and a lower carbon footprint. You deserve Viva CalleSJ. And now that the wheels are in motion, we all get to enjoy the surreal and exhilarating phenomenon that is Viva CalleSJ, too. So good job! Thanks!

vivacallesj.org

Good for families

TRY NOT TO DROOL ALL OVER THE SHOWROOM
AT THE SILICON VALLEY AUTO SHOW

The cars of tomorrow, the newest models, concept cars, gadgets for your favorite means of personal transportation, collectibles— spoiler alert—it's all there in shiny amazingness at the Silicon Valley Auto Show. I'm just going to need to ask those prone to excitable salivary episodes to please bring your ShamWow with you to avoid any embarrassing puddles. Pulling in huge crowds and an unbelievable list of vendors in a massive exhibit space, there's nothing small or understated about this show. It's the sexy beast of car shows to be sure. I repeat, for the safety of yourself and others, please see to your own spittle.

San Jose McEnery Convention Center, 150 W San Carlos St.,
San Jose, 95113
svautoshow.com

Good family activity

JAM WITH
THE SILICON VALLEY
ROLLER GIRLS

Flat track roller derby—it's just as exciting and empowering and fierce as you think it is, and it's happening in San Jose. The KillaBytes, Dot.Kamikazes, and the Hard Drivers are the league's A, B, and C teams, and these ladies . . . who am I kidding, they aren't ladies, not on the track they aren't. These women will blow you away with their speed and skill. If you haven't had a chance to see a bout before, there's nothing to worry about. It's easy to follow and the diehards who are most likely sitting near you will be happy to fill you in on the rules. Complete with fun names, colorful commentary, and the best uniforms of any sport, this is a special club with a cult following and shouldn't be missed.

Silicon Valley Roller Girls
svrollergirls.com

Good family activity

SENSE SERIOUS SEISMIC ACTIVITY
WITH THE SAN JOSE EARTHQUAKES

Call it soccer or football or footie, but any way you label it, the Quakes fans are rabid and the team is A+, making for an all-around brilliant time when you attend a home game. Combine the team's talent with Avaya Stadium's natural grass field, its gorgeous open air, and sustainable solar roof assets, and you really are living by California rules. The stadium also happens to be, in true geek city fashion, the first cloud-enabled professional sports stadium using next-generation tech to deliver the most engaging digital fan experience. Oh, and did I mention the stadium has the largest outdoor bar in North America? The 3,647-square-foot slab supports 45 beers on tap. Just thought I'd mention that. So what are you waiting for? Follow the Ultras' lead and chant along, "Goonies never say die!"

Avaya Stadium, 1123 Coleman Ave., San Jose, 95110
408-556-7700, sjearthquakes.com

Good family activity

DIVE HEAD FIRST
INTO THE SHARK TANK

While you might initially laugh at the idea of a city with such a warm climate having an NHL hockey team, San Jose bleeds teal for their Sharks and you will, too. With a rapscallion mascot (SJ Sharkie) who repels from the arena rafters and TPs visiting team fans (several of our home game traditions involve the *Jaws* theme), we might have the most fun of any fans during the regular season. Plus, we have the loudest fans in the league, and volume has to count for something, right? The Sharks consistently make it to the playoffs and are a class act organization on and off the ice. They may not have the number of Stanley Cups representative of their skill and fan loyalty (yet), but one home game and you'll see why the SAP Center is called the Shark Tank, even when it's hosting world-famous music acts.

SAP Center at San Jose, 525 W Santa Clara St., San Jose, 95113
408-999-5757, sharks.nhl.com

Good family activity

GET YOUR MOTOR RUNNIN'
AT HOT SAN JOSE NIGHTS

Gearheads get hoppin' when July rolls around, because that means it's time for hot rods, muscle cars, aircraft, food, music, and just a good ole time at Hot San Jose Nights. Collectors come out of the woodwork each year to display their vintage, restored beauties and talk a bit of shop. This is a super popular event with kids, and chairs and coolers are essential as there's a lot of ground to cover. Car people are some of the coolest, nicest folks around, and this event showcases not only some amazing machines but some of the most skilled and genuinely sweet, splendidly passionate people.

Reid-Hillview Airport, 2500 Cunningham Ave., San Jose, 95148
408-929-2256, hotsanjosenights.com

Good family activity

BAT A THOUSAND
WITH THE SAN JOSE GIANTS

A World Series ticket can be hard to come by, not to mention budget busting, but a chance to see championship players before they make it to the majors is a short, affordable walk. With an impressive team record and unusually accessible and friendly players, a San Jose Giants home game showcases the best of San Jose's no-ego, down-home vibe. Tim Lincecum, Buster Posey, Matt Cain, and Madison Bumgarner, to name a few, are all SJ Giants alums, and many kids have the autographs (signed before every game) to prove it. The stadium has you very close to the action and opts to forgo digital ads for fun traditions like the beer batter (when the designated "beer batter" from the opposing team strikes out, beer becomes half price!). A home run outing for kids and fans, a game is even a winner among the baseball apathetic.

Excite Ballpark, 588 E Alma Ave., San Jose, 95112
408-297-1435, sjgiants.com

Good family activity

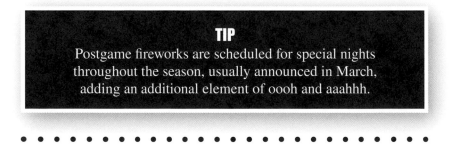

TIP
Postgame fireworks are scheduled for special nights throughout the season, usually announced in March, adding an additional element of oooh and aaahhh.

FLIP FOR THE TALENT
AT LAKE CUNNINGHAM
ACTION SPORTS PARK

If you want to see gravity being inexplicably defied, roll on over to Lake Cunningham Action Sports Park. At sixty-eight thousand square feet, LCRSP is the largest skatepark in California and features the world's largest cradle, tallest vert wall, largest full pipe, plus a totally rad variety of terrain for all skill levels. It's kind of like Leonardo DiCaprio in *Titanic*. You know, "I'm the king of the world!" If the park could talk, I'm pretty sure that's what it would say. The 8.5-acre bike park added in 2018 takes it to an 11 and really secured its place as a world-class facility. Watching boarders and bladers pivot and biff is not for the weak of heart, mind you, but it is exhilarating. If you aren't already a Tony Hawk in training, a visit to this place may be the gateway that gets you hooked. Participants might want to proactively make note of the nearest hospital, just in case a landing decides to nail you.

Lake Cunningham Action Sports Park, 2305 S White Rd., San Jose, 95101
408-793-5510, tinyurl.com/LCASP

Good family activity

SCORE A TOUR
OF LEVI'S STADIUM

Levi's Stadium set the bar very high as a standout stadium experience. So high it hosted Super Bowl 50. Yes, the 49ers scored big time with the smartest and greenest stadium in the NFL. Even if you don't get to see a game here, the tour is a pleasure for both the football fan and the geek. Should you fall into the overlapping section of that Venn diagram, you may need to pace yourself so you don't overheat. Tours of Levi's give the uber-fan an unprecedented, behind-the-scenes look at all the tech and innovation that you'd expect from the Silicon Valley. There's a whole lot of awesome here. Combine your guided tour of the stadium with the twenty-thousand-square-foot 49ers Museum and explore the eleven galleries and exhibit spaces housing, among other things, five glorious Lombardi Super Bowl championship trophies.

Levi's Stadium, 4900 Marie P. Debartolo Way, Santa Clara, 95054
415-464-9377, levisstadium.com

Light Rail, vta.org

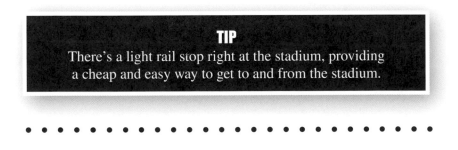

TIP
There's a light rail stop right at the stadium, providing a cheap and easy way to get to and from the stadium.

SEE THE NEXT X GAMES CHAMP
TUCK A NO HANDER AT CALABAZAS BMX PARK

A beautiful park of its own accord, Calabazas also happens to have the largest city-funded BMX course of its kind in the Bay Area, with few rivals in the rest of California. Bring your bikes if you count yourself among the dexterous and revel in the extremeness of it all. For those of you who feel a tad misclassified as land mammals and have put coordination on your birthday wish list more than a few years, there are benches on which you can channel your powers of extreme spectating. Mad bike skills seem to grow like weeds out here, and most days you can find groups of brave athletes practicing their moves in this sweetest of spots.

Calabazas Park, Rainbow Dr. and Blaney Ave., San Jose, 95129
sanjose.org/listings/calabazas-park

Good family activity

RIDE THE GIANT CONCRETE SLIDES
AT BRIGADOON PARK

Life is short, and sometimes the greatest joys and the most memorable moments are those with their foundation in silly, simple, childish whims. There are 193 parks in San Jose, each with its own perks and personality, and Brigadoon Park is no exception. Carved into the sides of the park's hill are massive concrete slides. When perched upon a piece of cardboard (which often can be found at the base of the slide, left for community use), you can reach some remarkable speeds. It's a slide. It's not a lap in a NASCAR race car, and it's a bit of a trek to the top, but it's a fun little exercise that is free, simple, and guaranteed to put a smile on your face.

Brigadoon Park, Brigadoon Way and Maloney Drive, San Jose, 95121
sanjose.org/listings/brigadoon-park

Good family activity

STOP AND SMELL THE ROSES
AT THE MUNICIPAL AND HERITAGE ROSE GARDENS

There are those in the "every rose has its thorn" camp, and then there are those who know anytime you can place yourself in the middle of thousands of rose bushes, it's a pretty awesome day. The Heritage Rose Garden and Municipal Rose Garden are colorful and unexpected floral gems that thrive in San Jose's urban setting. Acres and literally thousands of blooms burst with color and fill the air with fragrance at these two gardens of paradise.

Heritage Rose Garden, Spring and Taylor Sts., San Jose, 95110
heritageroses.us

Municipal Rose Garden, Naglee Ave. and Dana Ave., San Jose, 95126
408-794-7275, sanjose.org/MRoseGarden

Good family activity

GET CONNECTED TO NATURE THROUGH PLAY
AT HAPPY HOLLOW PARK AND ZOO

With its puppet theater and its kiddie rides, this Association of Zoos and Aquariums–accredited zoo is a visual feast for children, but the extraordinarily up-close viewing of rare animals appeals to the youngster in all of us. This intimate zoo exhibits a specially-curated collection of highly threatened and endangered species employing incredible ingenuity which provides visitors with optimal vantage points for observation and education. Around each corner is a surprise in the form of lemurs, wallaby, or giant anteaters. Happy Hollow was also the first zoo and amusement park to be LEED Gold certified, so it's fun to see the park's solar power, water runoff collection systems, and vegetated roofs at play as you explore this locally adored icon.

Happy Hollow Park and Zoo, 1300 Senter Rd., San Jose, 95112
408-794-6400, hhpz.org

Good family activity

TIP

Honey from the Happy Hollow beehive is harvested by the local 4-H club and beekeeping class members. The honey is then sold in the giftshop with all proceeds going to support mountain gorillas in Virunga National Park, one of the zoo's global conservation partners. Pick some up in the store for a sweet deal!

GET FIT TO A TEE TIME
AT CINNABAR HILLS GOLF CLUB

A game of golf can be made or broken by the course, the company, and the weather. While I can't do a thing about the company you keep, I will point out that San Jose's weather is sunny, on average, three hundred days a year. Combine that fact with the picturesque, quintessentially California view from the Cinnabar Hills Golf Club, plus its champion-caliber courses, and you have a pretty good chance of achieving two out of three. Choose between the club's three nine-hole courses—the Canyon, the Lake, or the Mountain. Even the non-golfer—you know, the one you dragged along—will be wooed by the lush hilly views, wild turkeys, hawks, and even deer. From sunrise to sunset, this magical place is one you can easily relish. I'd bet my nine-iron on it.

Cinnabar Hills Golf Club, 23600 McKean Rd., San Jose, 95141
408-323-7814, cinnabarhills.com

TIP
Don't miss the fantastic collection of golf artifacts in the Lee Brandenburg Historical Golf Museum located inside the clubhouse free of admission.

GO SEASONAL
AT ALUM ROCK PARK

It's been said that San Jose doesn't have any real seasons, and while our awesome weather is relatively constant, there are lovely places to experience the gentle California transitions much more dramatically. Alum Rock Park, the first municipal park in California, is one of these places. This wild and rustic park with thirteen miles of trails is set on 720 acres. With the east-west and south sides of the park on opposite sides of a canyon, the two halves see a whole different set of flora and fauna, making it possible to see major changes from one week to the next. Various wildflowers in spring, flowing creeks and striking green hills in the winter, golden brown grasses in the summer, and foliage change in autumn make this a park for all seasons.

Alum Rock Park, 15350 Penitencia Creek Rd., San Jose, 95127
408-794-7275, sanjose.org/listings/alum-rock-park

Good family activity

PEAK YOUR INTEREST AND YOUR HEART RATE
ON MOUNT UMUNHUM

Want to hike a moderate 7.7 miles with 1,150 feet of continuous gain at an average 6% grade to a circa 1957 radio tower that sits on a summit at 3,486 feet? Would you also like stunning views of other Bay Area peaks and a Native American ceremonial space? I suspected as much. You're in luck! Locals who rebelliously spent the '80s and '90s trespassing onto Mount Umunhum (and law-abiding visitors brand new to the famous landmark) can now access the summit legally, respectfully, and safely, plus get a decent workout and history lesson in the process, thanks to one of the newest trails to open in San Jose. Taking a hard pass on the whole hiking for hours portion of this recreational option? Fair enough; you can cheat and drive 99% of the way there and just tackle the final 160 stairs to the top. The tower itself is off limits due to unfortunate amounts of lead in the aging paint, but the climb (be it the full or abbreviated version) is definitely well worth the effort. Download the Stories of Mount Umunhum Audio Tour for a clever way to help take your mind off the most difficult parts of the climb.

Mount Umunhum at Sierra Azul Open Space Preserve
openspace.org/mount-umunhum-sierra-azul

● ●

TIP

The Mt. Umunhum trailhead is located at the Bald Mountain parking area in the Sierra Azul Open Space Preserve. Mount Umunhum is ONLY accessible via Hicks Road to Mt. Umunhum Road. Do not take any other route that may be recommended by online maps and/or your GPS device.

CONQUER THE LONGEST LEG
OF THE COYOTE CREEK TRAIL

The Coyote Creek Trail is one of the longest trail systems, extending from the bay to San Jose's southern boundary and beyond. The southern reach goes from Tully Road to Morgan Hill, near Anderson County Park, and measures 16.8 miles. While not terribly difficult with regard to climb, it is a good distance, and making the thirty-three-mile round-trip certainly earns you a big dinner. It's a challenge on bike and even more so on foot, but you'll see all manner of transportation taking on this popular paved pathway. The trail is a birdwatchers' paradise, and as you make your way along the wild creek, you'll spy heron, egret, woodpeckers, hawks, and even ospreys as you approach Morgan Hill.

Coyote Creek Trail
sanjose.org/listings/coyote-creek-trail

Humane Society Silicon Valley
hssv.org/volunteer/doggy-day-out, doggydayout@hssv.org

TIP

The Humane Society Silicon Valley (located in neighboring Milpitas) offers a furbulous Doggy Day Out program for those who'd like to treat a large, adoptable shelter dog to a morning hike. If you aren't up for the entire stretch, you can take on a smaller portion with a pooch companion. The walk will help the canine get some good, stress-reducing sniffs in and adds an adorable fur-factor to your own walk. It's a win-win. And, who knows, maybe you'll make a four-legged love connection!?

SCARE YOURSELF SILLY
WITH A FLASHLIGHT TOUR OF THE WINCHESTER MYSTERY HOUSE, IF YOU DARE

It's only one of the most famous and most haunted houses in the world. But you can handle all the stories of documented paranormal activity surrounding the home of Sarah Winchester, heir to the Winchester rifle fortune. You're not the least bit scared to walk the halls of this massive (and quite beautiful) home. I can tell, when you walk up a staircase that just stops, you aren't going to lose it. And I'm sure you won't have a problem when you come to doors that open to brick walls. Now, how about if you did all of that at night, with the house lights out and only a flashlight to guide you? And what if it were Friday the 13th? Or Halloween night? Changes the whole setup now, doesn't it? Well, what's the holdup? Chicken?

Winchester Mystery House, 525 S Winchester Blvd., San Jose, 95128
408-247-2101, winchestermysteryhouse.com

Good family activity

TIP

The winter holidays see the house and grounds decked out with lights and Victorian-style decorated trees, bringing out an entirely different kind of spirit. And don't let the fame of the house force you to overlook the gardens. The grounds are immaculately kept, and it's worth a look, especially if you are botanically inclined.

CELEBRATE THE HOLIDAYS
SAN JOSE STYLE

It's just a three-hour drive from San Jose to a snow lover's paradise, but real San Jose natives bask in the glow of a mild and even sunny winter full of ice skating under palm trees, nostalgic animatronic holiday displays, and carnival rides. From November to early January, downtown smells like warm churros, fresh kettle corn, and evergreens. The city knows how to close out a calendar year.

Downtown Ice, Circle of Palms, 127 S Market St., San Jose, 95113
downtownicesj.com

Christmas in the Park, 101 West Santa Clara St., San Jose, 95113
408-200-3800, christmasinthepark.com

Winter Wonderland, winterwonderlandsj.com

Good family activity

The **Downtown Ice rink at the Circle of Palms** is not only an incredible opportunity to skate without a coat, but a feat of engineering befitting our metropolis. Built each year for two months of skating, the LED light displays are programmed to the music playing while you glide under the fronds.

Across from the ice rink, **Christmas in the Park** takes over all of Cesar Chavez Park. With music (both live and piped-in holiday classics), hundreds of small trees decorated by community groups, moving displays, a stage for local performers, and lights, lights, and more lights, it's as festive a place as you'll ever find and chock full of families taking it all in.

Winter Wonderland is adjacent to Christmas in the Park and dots the nearby paseos and parts of the park with an assortment of carnival rides. open late, some of the rides give you a stunning bird's-eye view of all the lights and stars at night.

GO FULL FLORAL OVERLOAD
AT NOLA'S IRIS GARDEN

For just six weeks in April and May, Nola invites visitors to stroll through her sincerely spectacular five acres of gardens where more than two thousand varieties of iris explode with color. The viewing garden, which sits on forty-five acres of private ranch (including a more than one-hundred-year-old ranch house), is genuinely breathtaking set among rolling hills dotted with horses. Friendly barn cats and only slightly less friendly chickens roam the property freely, adding to the distinct charm of this remarkable hidden gem. The abundance of ancient farm equipment, kitsch statuary, and rusty junkyard treasures that are scattered about the property is in stark contrast to the overwhelming elegance of the peak blossom, but this juxtaposition really just enhances the overall allure of the destination. Nola's is a truly inspiring demonstration of how sharing one's personal passions really can spark joy in others.

Nola's Iris Garden, 4195 Sierra Rd., San Jose, 95132
408-258-2611, walking-p-bar.com

Chateau CharMarron Peony Gardens, 5335 Sierra Rd., San Jose, 95132
408-251-7048, 4peonies.com

Good for families

TIP

In need of an even bigger floral fix? Just up the road from Nola's is Chateau CharMarron Peony Gardens, with more than 240 varieties showing off their epic brilliance from late March to early June. Be sure to sample their hand-picked, estate grown and bottled, 100% virgin olive oil during your visit, too.

GET COCKY
AT EMMA PRUSCH FARM REGIONAL PARK

Upon parking at Emma Prusch Farm, you'll be greeted by chickens. And these chickens, along with an inordinate number of roosters, will very likely seduce you with their extensive range of clucks and chortles. As you make your way toward the grass and barn, you'll realize there are scores of the most ridiculously beautiful chickens you have ever seen roaming free without a care in the world. And you will likely have never seen so many different kinds of chickens in your life. Every color, shape, and size, all getting along great, making you want to be a chicken. Can't we all just be chickens? Then you will see a dozen or so peacocks just walking around in the open, perching in trees and on fences and picnic tables. You might conclude you've died and arrived at your eternal reward. It's that wonderful. Stay for the kite flying, 4-H happenings, and the historic orchard, but come for the exemplary roosters and peacocks.

Emma Prusch Farm Regional Park, 647 S King Rd., San Jose, 95116
408-794-6262, pruschfarmpark.org

Andy's Pet Shop
51 Notre Dame Ave., San Jose, 95113
408-297-0840, andyspetshop.com

Good family activity

TIP

Need an exotic bird excursion upgrade? Behold the majesty of Ruby the resident Macaw (as well as an impressive array of adoptable pigeons, doves, and flightless reptiles, rodents and felines) at Andy's Pet Shop. Andy's has been in operation since 1950 and stocks their adoption center with 100% non-profit rescue group animals.

HOST THE PERFECT PICNIC
IN THE PASTORAL PASTURES OF THE
SIERRA VISTA OPEN SPACE PRESERVE

On the "back" side of Alum Rock Park, you will find one of the most peaceful preserves in the greater Bay Area with some of the most stunning views of Silicon Valley. Within the Sierra Vista Open Space Preserve (which has many options for all levels of hikers, mountain bikers, and equestrians alike), there's a single trail that leads to perhaps the most excellent of all picnic tables. There it sits in its singular isolation not far into The Aquila Loop Trail. It sits silently as you might expect a table to do, very much in the moment, overlooking a grassy pasture stippled with rocky geology once part of the ocean floor. Like Epicurus, this table embraces the simple pleasures of life and invites you to do exactly the same. *Aquila* is Latin for "hawk," and the perfect thermals of this particular trail location almost guarantee that you'll see a variety of raptors making lazy circles in the sky, adding peace and awe to this special slice of Zen. But it's not just the rustic natural environment surrounding this eating surface that makes it so perfect for picnicking; as an added bonus, quite frequently you will be wandering and noshing amongst a herd of cows. I hear you scoff confusedly, but trust me, cows are the new goat, and there's no better way to forget you're minutes from

● ●

the 10th largest city in the United States than consuming fresh baguettes beside bucolic bovines. It's a fabulously bizarre twist on romantic that nourishes all the essential life basics: time in nature, light exercise, sustenance, and cows. Did I mention the cows? It's utterly idyllic.

Sierra Vista Open Space Preserve, 5341 Sierra Rd., San Jose, 95132
openspaceauthority.org/visitors/preserves/sierra

Good for families

WITNESS A WHOLE LOT OF DOGS
HAVING THEIR DAY AT BARK IN THE PARK

Unleash your inner hound and sniff out the ultimate treat for doggie devotees. Each September, Bark in the Park provides a variety of canine competitions, copious belly rubs, and some prime slobbering opportunities. I'm not going to lie, there's also quite a bit of butt sniffing among the four-legged attendees. This is a no-judgment event, however, so it's all good at this gathering of pooches and their people. Don't have a dog? No worries. That just translates into more free hands for petting and throwing Frisbees! Tail wagging, costume, and owner/dog look-alike contests are just a few of the events you can look forward to at this all-day festival. Added bonus? All proceeds benefit the Campus Community Association and local pet charities.

Bark in the Park, William Street Park, William and S 16th Sts.,
San Jose, 95112
barksanjose.org

Good family activity

GIDDYUP
AT GARROD FARMS AND
COOPER-GARROD ESTATE VINEYARDS

What better way to get into the spirit of the West than on a horse? Garrod Farms, in the hills of neighboring Saratoga, provides some superb views of San Jose during the hour-long trail rides. Rides can be arranged as early as 8:30 a.m., seven days a week, and all levels of riders can be accommodated. For extra fun do the ninety-minute trail ride first thing Saturday or Sunday morning (8:30 a.m.) or the wine tasting ride, which occurs on the last Sunday of the month and includes a wine tasting after your ride at the historic 120-acre Cooper-Garrod Estate Vineyard. Inside the tasting room, aviation aficionados will want to see the photo exhibit of George Cooper's career as a NASA test pilot. Additionally, you can take an extensive tour with the winemakers on certain days, an ecotour/hike through the vineyard's ecosystem, or just tour the facilities on your own.

Garrod Farms, 22647 Garrod Rd., Saratoga, 95070
408-867-9527, garrodfarms.com

Cooper-Garrod Estate Vineyards, 22645 Garrod Rd., Saratoga, 95070
877-923-4616, cgv.com

FIND YOUR INNER CHILD
AT THE CHILDREN'S
DISCOVERY MUSEUM

It's no wonder we have more baby geniuses per capita than anywhere else in the world. Okay, maybe that's not a totally accurate statistic, but when Steve Wozniak invests in a museum for kids, you better believe it's going to be one that will wow and entertain as well as educate. It also might be where tech companies recruit their future engineers or where your child (or a legitimately borrowed child) discovers his or her own interests and talents. The museum caters expertly to all age groups (even under one) and to all the senses. Fostering curiosity and a love for lifelong learning is at the core of each of the exhibits in this 52,000-square-foot cultural pearl, so be prepared to come back again and again and again.

Children's Discovery Museum, 180 Woz Way, San Jose, 95110
408-298-5437, cdm.org

Good family activity

FISH FOR A STRIKE
AT UNCLE BUCK'S FISH BOWL AND GRILL

Bowling is fun, but underwater-themed bowling is dolphin-itely better. Bass Pro Shops is absolutely krilling it, with their magnificently detailed and immersive undersea inspired bowling lanes. Uncle Buck's Fish Bowl and Grill is a camp treat whale worth waiting for, though wait you may well do. Reservations are not taken except for private events, and lines on the weekends can be as long as four hours (patience training for the fishing life I guess). Get there early and keep casting your net if you don't catch a break first try. Don't be koi or clam up, just grab a meal at the grill or explore the ginormous store while you wait for the tide to turn in your favor. If you happen to be waiting around noon on Saturday, you can help get in the right frame of mind by watching staff feed the giant sturgeon, bass, catfish, and carp in the shop's 14,000-gallon aquarium with waterfall. The added ocean ambiance will have you hooked.

Bass Pro Shops, 5160 Cherry Ave., San Jose, 95118
669-234-5600, unclebucksfishbowlandgrill.com/bowling

stores.basspro.com/us/ca/san-jose/5160-cherry-ave.html

Good family activity

CULTURE AND HISTORY

HONOR THOSE WHO SERVED
AT THE VETERANS DAY PARADE

You will be hard-pressed to find a more moving event than the San Jose Veterans Day Parade presented each year by the United Veterans Council of Santa Clara County in partnership with the city. Since 1919, an opportunity to see and hear first-hand the sacrifices made by our servicemen and servicewomen has been provided in the form of this parade. It is a ceremony with floats, music, marching, military vehicles, and plenty of celebration, but it also carries with it a lot of heart, honor, history, pride, and pain, so bring your tissues and your gratitude. The stories told and the guests who share at the memorial ceremony preceding the commencement of the parade will leave an indelible mark.

Veterans Day Parade, Downtown San Jose, uvcscc.org

Good family activity

STOMP GRAPES
AT THE LEGENDARY ITALIAN FAMILY FESTA

For a weekend you can be part of one big familia! Join dreamy tenors, the Fratello Marionettes, and the entire Italian community at the Italian Family Festa held each August. Play bocce ball, partake at the wine garden, delight in culinary demonstrations, join in traditional folk dancing (oh, you will be asked to join in at some point, you can count on it), and prepare yourself for . . . So. Much. Food. Taking the prize for one of the most anticipated events of the entire festa is the Grape Stomp. Dress up in your best Lucille Ball digs (or not) and get your feet wet in an actual barrel of grapes. This contest sees teams of two (one stomping and one keeping the juices flowing into the jug) competing for the title of "Brava Squadra D'Uva."

Italian Family Festa
408-368-9094, italianfamilyfestasj.org

Little Italy, W Julian and N Almaden Blvd., San Jose, 95110
littleitalysj.com

Good family activity

DISCOVER
ONE OF THE LAST THREE REMAINING JAPANTOWNS IN THE UNITED STATES

San Jose's bustling Japantown artfully fuses its long history and beautiful heritage with a tight, active community, creating a colorful city district popular with both locals and tourists. Authentic Japanese restaurants, art galleries, a year-round farmers market, and specialty shopping thrive here, and stores that have been in operation for over one hundred years are fixed right next to the newest hangouts. Stores selling traditional bonsai, Japanese string instruments, and kimonos, interspersed with an organic dog treat shop, premier sneaker consignment store, and a tattoo parlor make this an outstanding place to spend the day exploring. You never know what to expect here, except of course a great time.

Japantown, near 5th and Jackson, San Jose, 95112
jtown.org

Japanese American Museum, 535 N 5th St., San Jose, 95112
408-294-3138, jamsj.org

Good family activity

TIP

For a really moving experience, take a tour of the Japanese American Museum led by an internment camp survivor.

WALK LIKE AN EGYPTIAN
AT THE ROSICRUCIAN MUSEUM

Indiana Jones and Laura Croft have nothing on you, because you have the Rosicrucian on your side and the Rosicrucian is home to the largest collection of Egyptian artifacts in western North America. With four thousand artifacts, a replica tomb, a planetarium, and an alchemy garden, you're in for an education fit for a pharaoh. This is no pyramid scheme; even the museum itself was modeled after the Temple of Amon at Karnak. Special lectures and kids' activities are scheduled a few times during the day, so check the schedule first thing so you don't miss anything you might want to participate in.

Rosicrucian Museum, 1660 Park Ave., San Jose, 95191
408-947-3635, egyptianmuseum.org

Good family activity

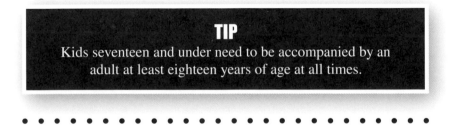

TIP
Kids seventeen and under need to be accompanied by an adult at least eighteen years of age at all times.

MARVEL AT THE MAJESTY
OF THE CATHEDRAL BASILICA
OF ST. JOSEPH

The Cathedral Basilica of St. Joseph has taken a licking and kept on ticking, suffering earthquake damage, fires, and a total of five iterations previous to 1885. Made a minor basilica by Pope John Paul II in 1997 in recognition of its beauty, history, and service, this beloved city landmark is one of perseverance and splendor. If you think the exterior is magnificent, just wait until you step inside and discover the exceptional craftsmanship of its thirty-nine stained glass windows, some of which were created in Germany with mouth-blown Bavarian glass made from a formula dating back to the eleventh century. An ornate altar and painted frieze add to the grandeur of the cathedral as do the spellbinding acoustics. If you can catch one of many public concerts held there, it's an unforgettable feeling.

Cathedral Basilica of St. Joseph, 80 S Market St., San Jose, 95113
408-283-8100, stjosephcathedral.org

GO ADOBE TO ADOBE
WITH WALKS AND TALKS

One of the city's best resources is San Jose State University, and one of the most educational and fun ways for a visitor (or resident) to get a feel for San Jose's layout and legacies is with a Walks and Talks tour. Keen young SJSU students lead you on a professional, structured, but light and fun tour lasting about an hour. From the Peralta Adobe (San Jose's first historic landmark) to technology giant Adobe's headquarters, this tour illuminates the innovative spirit that drove the pioneers here hundreds of years ago and is still so present in the city. The synergy of the old and new (given by the next generation of citizens) will have you smiling as will some of the historical accounts and rarely divulged city secrets. In addition to their regular tours, keep an eye out for the very popular Breweries, Bars & Brothels Tour which will open your eyes to a far more scandalous San Jose. Tours focusing on Cesar Chavez's local legacy and Holiday themed tours are also a valuable way to gain insight into this City's origins and evolution.

Walks and Talks start and end locations depend on the tour
sanjosewalksandtalks.org

GET IN THE SPIRIT
AT THE ROSE, WHITE & BLUE PARADE

For a town of a million, San Jose still has lot of small-town qualities and simpler time feels. One endearing display of these types of unaffected sensibilities is the annual Rose, White & Blue Parade, which takes place on the Fourth of July along the Alameda and surrounding Shasta/Hanchett and Rose Garden neighborhoods. In a fun throwback to days gone by, you can watch streamer-decorated wagons carrying costumed pets, vintage autos, horses, floats, local school marching bands—all the things you'd expect from a tiny town parade. Okay, so there might be a few iPads snapping photos as the parade passes by, and past grand marshals have included modern tech celebrity Steve Wozniak, but aside from that you'd think you were miles away from the capital of Silicon Valley. Stick around for the picnic, car show, dancing, live music, and artists' booths.

Rose, White & Blue Parade
rosewhiteblueparade.com

Good family activity

LIVE IN THE PAST
AT HISTORY PARK AT KELLEY PARK

At the south end of Kelley Park sits a charming mix of twenty-seven original and reproduction homes. Many of the buildings house small museums including the Chinese American Historical Museum at the Ng Shing Gung, the Portuguese Historical Museum at the Impario, the African American Heritage House at Zanker House, and the Museum of the Boat People and Republic of Vietnam at the Greenwalk House. A blacksmith shop, old gas station, stables, a trolley barn (with free historic trolley rides), a print shop, and even an ice cream parlor (best malts ever) make up fourteen acres of the most fabulous Throwback Thursday you ever saw. Far enough from road sounds, History Park really does take you back to the early 1900s. Tours (given on weekdays) are very informative and there are plenty of places to picnic and soak up a bit of the past.

Entrance located at 635 Phelan Ave., San Jose, 95112
408-287-2290, historysanjose.org

Spirit of '45
spiritof45.org

Good family activity

TIP

Many organizations host events at History Park and one of the most magical is the Spirit of '45 Swing Dance each August commemorating the end of WWII. Attendees of all ages sport their victory curls and glam '40s fashion, surrounded by vintage vehicles and military tents, while a Big Band serenades the dancing crowd under a canopy of stars and the glow of the 115-foot electric light tower.

GET IN THE RIGHT STATE OF "MINE"
AT ALMADEN QUICKSILVER COUNTY PARK & MINING MUSEUM

An old mercury mine and a museum honoring its past might seem about as fun as touring Chernobyl at first, but once you put away your fear of blood poisoning or falling down a deserted mine shaft, this outing will likely make its way up to the top of your list. The part mining played in San Jose's history, the immigrant labor and its economic impact, is all well documented at the museum and is really a fascinating account many locals don't even know about. It's a niche excursion for sure, but between exploring the vast scenery of the park and the museum itself, it's an easy full day of historical hiking.

Almaden Quicksilver County Park & Mining Museum, 21350 Almaden Rd., San Jose, 95120
408-323-1107, newalmaden.org/AQSPark

Hacienda Cemetery, 21440 Bertram Rd., San Jose, 95120
californiapioneers.com/visit/hacienda-cemetery

● ●

REST IN PIECES?

The 1898 grave of thirteen-year-old Richard Bertram Barrett's left arm (detached from poor Richard via a hunting accident) can be found in the southern (uphill) portion of the Hacienda Cemetery, which sits just behind the Mining Museum. The cemetery is private property, but permission to respectfully explore is typically granted with advanced request through the California Pioneers website.

SHOPPING AND FASHION

GET ADDICTED
TO LIFE ON THE ROW AT SANTANA ROW

Attention, shopping zealots! Santana Row, the city's undisputed premiere shopping destination, is calling you. Pick up already! With its comfortable blend of high-end, accessible, and niche stores, plus several salons and spas to cater to your exhausted, post-shopping-marathon bodies, it's not just recreation—it's a way of life. The indoor and sidewalk dining options are chic and plentiful, providing an array of stops for refueling, relaxing, and for showing off your new purchases. This boutique, balconied paradise, reminiscent of European fashion districts, is beautiful in and of itself, only adding to the likelihood that you may never want to leave. If that's the case, if another day (or two) is in order, no problem: the centrally located Hotel Valencia can accommodate those who still have some credit cards needing love.

Santana Row, 377 Santana Row, San Jose, 95128
408-551-4611, santanarow.com

TREASURE HUNT
ON SAN JOSE'S ANTIQUE ROW

Part museum, part shopping, and all awesome, San Jose is an antique junkie's paradise. Even the casual hobbyist and the newbie antique-curious will have a field day walking San Jose's Antiques Row. Dozens of stores along West San Carlos Street, spanning several blocks, are each packed to the gills with a history told in knickknacks, hat racks, lamps, books, pots, jewelry, clothes, furniture, and probably the idol from the first Indiana Jones movie. Whether you're looking for something specific or just looking, start at the Antiques Colony, a collection of fifty quality dealers in a nine-thousand-square-foot showroom and the largest antique collective in Silicon Valley. It is the anchor store for the rest of the row and will help steer you in the right direction based on your wants or needs. Take your time looking, and if you happen to find that perfect thing or things, prepare to negotiate!

The Antiques Colony, 1881 W San Carlos St., San Jose, 95128
408-293-9844, antiquescolony.com

Memory Lane Antiques, 1867 W San Carlos St., San Jose 95128
408-289-1022

Briarwood Antiques & Collectibles, 1885 W San Carlos St., San Jose, 95128
408-292-1720

Burbank Antiques, 1893 W San Carlos St., San Jose, 95128
408-292-3204

AWAKEN THE WHIMSICAL BOOKWORM WITHIN
AT HICKLEBEE'S BOOKSTORE

It's no secret we like a good book in San Jose. We also really like anything that appears to reverse the effects of aging. Enter Hicklebee's Bookstore, which cleverly disguises itself as a totally amazeballs children's bookstore, but in fact doubles as literary Botox. One "injection" of this precious store's impossibly whimsical decor and exposure to its comprehensive, carefully curated collection of children's literature, and you'll find yourself sitting on the floor excitedly anticipating tales of taco eating dragons and creepy anthropomorphic carrots. This cherished establishment uses colorful, chimerical mise-en-scène superbly. Its timelessly delightful, endlessly enchanting, and exceedingly inviting layout has the power to capture the imagination of dormant bookworms of any age, coax them to the surface, and instantly rekindle youth presumed lost long ago. Skip the spa and head to Hicklebee's for a rejuvenating wander through nooks of books and crannies. Oh, and the small humans under sixteen will also totally dig it, too, because books rock.

Hicklebee's Bookstore, 1378 Lincoln Ave., San Jose, 95125
408-292-8880, hicklebees.com

Good for families

VISIT VINYL PARADISE

You don't have to miss the days of flipping through records, admiring the cover art, nor do you have to miss listening to that non-replicable sound of a needle on vinyl. True, the musical trip down memory lane is less and less accessible in general these days, but San Jose holds on to its old and showcases it alongside all our shiny new. The city is a proud leader of the resurrection of vinyl popularity, which sees small local businesses supporting other small businesses. More and more, bars and restaurants are fixing up their record players and are choosing vinyl over streaming. Vintage vinyl DJ nights are increasingly popular too, and Streetlight Records and Needle to the Groove are two of the go-to places for hard-to-find, rare, mint condition records. Rediscover this lost art from the center of the movement taking place at these shops. They'll spin you right round, baby, right round.

Streetlight Records, 980 S Bascom Ave., San Jose, 95128
888-330-7776, streetlightrecords.com

Needle to the Groove, 410 E Santa Clara St., San Jose, 95113
408-418-3151, needletothegroove.net

ANSWER THE CALL
OF YOUR INNER INTERNATIONAL FASHIONISTA AT THE AO DAI FESTIVAL

A lavish display unlike any other, the annual Ao Dai Festival is, in a word, gorgeous. A celebration of Vietnamese art and culture, fashion (the Ao Dai is the long gown and pants traditionally worn by women in Vietnam) is at the center of this event, and it is absolutely stunning. Designers from Vietnam as well as the region are tasked with promoting the grace and beauty of Vietnamese women, and the results and artistic display of the fashion are just exquisite. Silks flow, golden threads glow, and grace is exhibited from head to toe each May. You'll be hard-pressed to find a more elegant and unique fashion event in the Bay Area.

Ao Dai Festival
aodaifestival.com

TIP
While the main fashion show is a paid event (with proceeds going to help orphans in Vietnam), you can catch one hundred models, along with stilt walkers, music, and a dragon dance for free, preceding the gala.

SCRATCH THAT SHOPPING ITCH
AT THE SAN JOSE FLEA MARKET

Vintage bicycle parts? Sure. A couch you swear was in your grandmother's house? Probably. Every kind of produce known to man? Definitely. The glowing briefcase from Pulp Fiction? I'm not going to say no. You can pretty much find any item you desire at what remains the largest open-air flea market in America. It might take you a bit to get through the 120 acres of booths selling everything from palm trees to perfumes, but if you can walk it, you can probably find it. This family tradition since 1960 may even have unsold items from the first day the market opened! You might even stumble across R2D2 or the treasure of Sierra Madre! Make sure you charge your smartphone before entering the flea, just in case you get lost.

San Jose Flea Market, 1590 Berryessa Rd., San Jose, 95133 408-453-1110, sjfm.com

The Garden at the Flea gardenattheflea.com

Good family activity

TIP
2019 saw a locally-driven live music stage, food truck area, and craft beer garden added to the pulgas. The Garden at the Flea invites you to catch a rad band, take in a tap takeover, and overall add more weeee to your flea.

MIND THE GEEK

GET YOUR GEEK ON
AT THE TECH INTERACTIVE

An exemplary model of geeky awesomeness, the Tech Interactive
has an aptly named interactive appeal that has kids and adults of
all ages making their techy pilgrimages over and over. Hands-on
exhibits on genetics, space, music, biology, geology, and more
amaze and educate while simultaneously telling a uniquely San
Jose/ Silicon Valley story. So much of the technology at the
center of scientific breakthroughs has come from this valley, but
the technology used to exhibit these narratives is also in many
cases born right here. Be sure to get to the earthquake simulator,
the space jet pack chair, and don't miss catching an educational
film shown on the truly astounding and immersive IMAX.

The Tech Interactive, 201 S Market St., San Jose, 95113
408-294-8324, thetech.org

Good family activity

SHOOT FOR THE STARS
AT LICK OBSERVATORY

Forget for a moment that planets have been discovered with the telescopes at Lick Observatory and just imagine what it took James Lick to build it. Maybe even cooler than viewing celestial bodies millions of light-years away from atop Mount Hamilton is the mind-blowing story of how a true visionary made it so. For starters, constructing a road to the summit of a mountain (4,209 feet above sea level) in the 1870s was no walk in the park. Navigating observatory materials (including huge telescope lenses shipped from Germany) through 365 turns, by horse, also was not easy. Any chance to visit this place is liable to blow your mind, but if you're visiting over a weekend from June to August and are lucky enough to get tickets, the "Music of the Spheres" series is by far the best "big bang" for your buck. A lecture by a leading scientist, two telescope viewings/tours, and a music concert all in one evening makes for a long, long night, but one that is truly out of this world.

Lick Observatory, 7281 Mt. Hamilton Rd., Mt. Hamilton, 95140
408-274-5061, ucolick.org

TOUR
THE GUADALUPE RIVER PARK LIKE A TRUE GEEK: BY SEGWAY

When in Rome, as they say, and when in San Jose, travel geek style because SJ born Nobel Prize-winning chemist Dudley R. Herschbach would want it that way. Besides feeling like you are the CEO of a startup during the dot-com boom while upon your trusty mechanical steed, the Segway is an easy and fun way to explore a large area for those who don't need to live the weekend-warrior lifestyle. With minimal effort you can soak up some sun, view tons of local wildlife, and learn a bit about the city. Tours start at the Tech Interactive (perfect for before or after a visit to the museum or the IMAX) and fill a couple of hours beautifully. Wave at Lupe, the Mammoth sculpture, as you zip by!

Guadalupe River Park Trail
grpg.org/river-park-gardens

Silicon Segway
650-355-8655, siliconsegway.com

Good family activity

GET ANIMATED
AT FANIME CON

Have you heard of the Japanese style of animation called anime? Did you know there's also a huge convention called FanimeCon, celebrating the tradition of anime, manga, and related arts and culture? Did you know it's been held for over twenty-five years in San Jose? Did you know that it attracts more than twenty thousand fans every year? Did you know that the cosplay is totally off the hook at the event? Did you also know that the city of San Jose officially declared May 23 Fanime Day in honor of the event, which takes over all of downtown and beyond? Well, now you know. The only thing left to do is go experience it for yourself.

San Jose McEnery Convention Center, 150 W San Carlos, San Jose, 95113
fanime.com

Good family activity

SPIN YOUR WHEELS
WITH SAN JOSE BIKE PARTY

Every month, delightfully madcap bike enthusiasts take to the streets for the San Jose Bike Party. Themed rides like Monsters vs. Aliens, Steampunk, and Mardi Gras see creatively costumed cyclists parading down city streets, music playing and lights flashing as they go. Themes are announced early on the website along with a playlist to get you pumped up, but actual routes remain secret until twenty-four hours before the party. Designated safety bikers called "birds" keep everyone safe, helping with directions and making sure rules of the road/ride are respected. The "ravens" cycle with large garbage cans in tow, dedicated to making sure no trash (feathers, streamers, food, etc.) is left behind. During the ride, participants flock en masse to a designated space where music, food trucks, and socializing commence. Combining imagination and eco-friendly transport, this all-ages event is a fine example of the typical, inclusive fun San Jose is teeming with.

Various locations
sjbikeparty.org

Good family activity

CHECK OUT
ONE OF THE COOLEST LIBRARIES EVER

Standing 136 feet tall with a footprint of over 475,000 square feet and containing 1.6 million volumes, the Dr. Martin Luther King Jr. Library is like the Andre the Giant of libraries. With eight floors full of quiet corners, views of the city, special collections, and even a telescope for viewing the city hall peregrine falcons, this joint venture between San Jose State University and the San Jose Public Library System is a sight to behold. From the giant digital book return tally as you enter, to the Ira F. Brilliant Center for Beethoven Studies and the Martha Heasley Cox Center for Steinbeck Studies, it's a learning space I bet literacy champion LeVar Burton would wholeheartedly endorse. Free one-hour tours of this glorious house of reading can be arranged ahead of time and occasionally can be accommodated on a drop-in basis.

Dr. Martin Luther King Jr. Library, 150 E San Fernando St., San Jose, 95112
408-808-2000, sjlibrary.org

FLOCK TO SEE
THE CITY HALL PEREGRINE FALCONS

Move over Kardashians! Clara and Fernando El Cohete, the City Hall peregrine falcons, have reached celebrity status few people, let alone birds, ever obtain. These two are part of an incredible survival story that saw the species recently come back from the brink of extinction, and as a result they have gathered quite the collection of fanbirds. The aviary soap opera unfolds eighteen stories above ground, and like any good reality show, the lens of a remotely operated camera transmits their every move. Highlights include courtship, mating, eggs arriving, hatching, banding day, fledgling and what appears to be a shocking nest-box eviction by a new falcon pair unfolding as this edition goes to print! The city is entranced February through June, with voter turnout never higher than when falcon baby name suggestions from local elementary school students are on the ballot. Fanbirds can be seen racing about in May, hoping for a glimpse of a successful first flight or, in the case of a fledgling fail, the opportunity to protect any fallen baby until a qualified scientist can inspect and transport it back to safety.

Nest Box, 200 E Santa Clara St., San Jose, 95113
408-535-4800, facebook.com/SanJoseCityHallFalcons

Good family activity

PASS GO
AND COLLECT $200 ON THE WORLD'S LARGEST MONOPOLY BOARD

If only there were a way to take one's love for board games and combine it with one's love of physical activity. If only there were a place where one could roll gigantic dice outside. If only there were a huge, record-breaking Monopoly board complete with all the houses, properties, and "Get Out of Jail Free" cards that I would need to play with my friends in the sun. I mean, I'd trade Marvin Gardens to have the opportunity to run about wearing a helmet with the Scottie dog Monopoly piece on it. Wait? You mean I can? There is? Wow! I feel like I just won second prize in a beauty contest!

Monopoly in the Park, 180 Woz Way, San Jose, 95110
monopolyinthepark.com

Good family activity

CELEBRATE THE GEEKIEST WEEK OF THE YEAR
WITH *STAR WARS* DAY
AND FREE COMIC BOOK DAY

During the first week in May, nerds, wonks, and geeks unite to honor the two dorkiest holidays in the dweeb canon—May the 4th (be with you), A.K.A. *Star Wars* Day and Free Comic Book Day, which occurs on the first Saturday in May. While *Star Wars* Day events across the city are in no short supply with even the most mainstream organizations trying to capitalize, there's only one true place the real *Star Wars* fans will be spending this sacred day—the *Star Wars* themed 7 Stars Bar & Grill. While EVERY day is technically *Star Wars* Day at 7 Stars, May the 4th sees roughly 10,000% more SW-themed costuming, trivia, drinks, memorabilia, raffle prizes, and an overall unabashed freak flag flying. Trust me, as sure as the Millennium Falcon made the Kessel Run in less than twelve parsecs, this wonderfully campy homage to a beloved and iconic movie franchise will more than satisfy your guilty pleasure requirement for the year.

As for Free Comic Book Day, it's exactly as awesome as it sounds, and there are numerous locations that participate in the name of literacy and geek philanthropy.

Good for families

7 Stars Bar & Grill
398 S Bascom Ave., San Jose, 95128
408-292-7827, 7starsbar.com

Legends Comics & Games
2200 Eastridge Loop, Ste 1085, San Jose, 95122
408-253-2643, legendscng.tcgplayerpro.com

Hijinx Comics
2050 Lincoln Ave., San Jose, 95125
408-266-1103, hijinxcomics.com

SpaceCat
1415 W San Carlos St., San Jose, 95126
superspacecat.com

FIGHT THE GOOD FIGHT
DURING THE FEATHERS OF FURY PILLOW FIGHT

It's a pretty amazing world we live in, where we can take some of our pent-up, fast-paced, digital stress and release it by smacking the holy living tar out of someone, in public, with a fully sanctioned, official pillow fight. It happens once a year in February, and the exact downtown location is only revealed twenty-four to thirty-six hours in advance. Why? Oh, we don't know; it's just more fun that way. And geekier because you have to keep checking Twitter or Facebook to get the details. Oh wait, we kind of do that already. Getting into the fray is fun and safe and totally family friendly. The feathers fly while some people try to curl up and sleep in the middle, and then everyone lends a hand cleaning up the feathers. Good times and sweet dreams.

Downtown San Jose
pillowfightsj.blogspot.com

Good family activity

FLY THE COOP
AT THE SILICON VALLEY TOUR DE COOP

It's a little known fact (but fact nonetheless) that the word *geek* used to refer to carnival workers who bit the heads off of live chickens in the name of entertainment. Happily, we have moved away from that archaic definition and by doing so allowed the everyday chicken enthusiast to adopt the moniker and celebrate in a less "decapitatious" geek fashion. The Silicon Valley Tour De Coop is a free, self-guided bicycle tour navigating participants to urban chicken coops, gardens, bee hives, hoop houses, and supremely hip and sustainable Silicon Valley homesteads. The annual September event is a total chick(en) magnet, attracting those interested in making their own backyards more flock-forward, as well as those happy to ride a route where they can meet new feathered (and nonfeathered) friends. Honey tastings, fresh lemonade, homemade candles, organic vegetables, sweets, and of course eggs are frequently available at many of the stops, so bring some cash and a backpack for your wares. While you can certainly chose alternative modes of transportation to cover the tour routes, admittedly it's much more geeky to bike so you can wear the cute little chicken-shaped bike helmet decorations that are available to download and assemble from the Tour De Coop website.

tourdecoop.org

Good for families

CREATE
MAGICAL MOMENTS
ESCAPING OMESCAPE'S
SORCERER'S SANCTUM

If extraterrestrials ever visited Earth, I wonder what they'd think of our species' sense of fun. Take the growing popularity of escape rooms for example. Essentially, you pay money to be locked with a bunch of people into a room, with no instructions, where you are then forced to argue about how to collaboratively solve puzzles in order to break out of said room, all within a strict time limit. When you break it down like that, it does seem like an odd pastime. Owning our oddities though is just another day as a San Josean, so it's no surprise we've cornered the market on imaginative escape rooms. Omescape is wildly popular for its quality puzzles, original plots, and a staff that really seems to enjoy their jobs. The Sorcerer's Sanctum scenario sees you accidentally stepping into a house occupied by great magicians and solving a series of magical puzzles in order to escape from the spell in time! No magic word is going to save you; you're going to have to work your wizardly wits collectively if you want to win. Once you've mastered the sanctum, try their other rooms: The Kingdom of Cats, Dark Altar, Joker's Asylum or Pandemic Zero.

Omescape, 625 Wool Creek Dr., Suite E, San Jose, 95112
408-622-0505, omescape.us/sanjose

SUGGESTED ITINERARIES

BROS AND BREWS

Join the Neighborhood At the Naglee Park Garage, 19

Sense Serious Seismic Activity with the San Jose Earthquakes, 69

Dive Head First into the Shark Tank, 70

Wet Your Whistle at Silicon Valley Beer Week, 34

Celebrate Oktoberfest Every Month at Teske's Germania, 24

Score a Tour of Levi's Stadium, 74

Share the Laughter at the San Jose Improv, 63

FAMILY FUN

Find Your Inner Child at the Children's Discovery Museum, 98

Get Connected to Nature through Play at Happy Hollow Park and Zoo, 78

Get Cocky at Emma Prusch Farm Regional Park, 92

Bat a Thousand with the San Jose Giants, 72

Get Your Geek on at the Tech Interactive, 124

Scare Yourself Silly with a Flashlight Tour of the Winchester Mystery House, if You Dare, 86

Awaken the Whimsical Bookworm within at Hicklebee's Bookstore, 118

Celebrate the Geekiest Week of the Year with *Star Wars* Day and Free Comic Book Day, 132

Fish for a Strike at Uncle Buck's Fish Bowl and Grill, 99

• •

FOOD ADVENTURER

GREAT DATE

GIRLS NIGHT OUT

• •

GLOBE TROTTER

LUXURY ESCAPE

MUSICAL MADNESS

OUTDOOR EXPLORER

THEATER GEEK

ACTIVITIES
BY MONTH

JANUARY

Try Not to Drool All Over the Showroom at the Silicon Valley Auto Show, 67

FEBRUARY

Get Reel at Cinequest Film Festival, 41

Fight the Good Fight during the Feathers of Fury Pillow Fight, 134

San Jose Jazz Winter Fest, 43

MARCH

Get Reel at Cinequest Film Festival, 41

San Jose Jazz Winter Fest, 43

APRIL

Stop and Smell the Roses at the Municipal and Heritage Rose Gardens, 77

Go Gull Floral Overload at Nola's Iris Garden, 90

MAY

Answer the Call of Your Inner International Fashionista at the Ao Dai Festival, 120

Flock to See the City Hall Peregrine Falcons, 130

Get Animated at FanimeCon, 127

Stop and Smell the Roses at the Municipal and Heritage Rose Gardens, 77

Go Gull Floral Overload at Nola's Iris Garden, 90

• •

Celebrate the Geekiest Week of the Year with *Star Wars* Day and Free
Comic Book Day, 132

JUNE

Eat Your Big, Fat, Greek Heart Out at the San Jose Greek Festival, 31

Walk the Walk at South First Fridays, 31

JULY

Get Your Motor Runnin' at Hot San Jose Nights, 71

Sample Teriyaki and Taiko at the Obon Festival, 25

Get in the Spirit at the Rose, White & Blue Parade, 109

Wet Your Whistle at Silicon Valley Beer Week, 34

AUGUST

Stomp Grapes at the Legendary Italian Family Festa, 103

Go All Access at the San Jose Jazz Summer Fest, 43

SEPTEMBER

Witness a Whole Lot of Dogs Having Their Day at Bark in the Park, 96

Chalk It Up to Awesome Art at the Luna Park Chalk Art Festival, 39

Bike, Blade, and Board at Viva CalleSJ, 66

OCTOBER

Scare Yourself Silly with a Flashlight Tour of the Winchester Mystery
House, If You Dare, 86

• •

NOVEMBER

DECEMBER

INDEX